To my superheroes, Avi and Noa.

May you always be as curious as you are today
and never stop asking questions.

{ ACCLAIM FOR **NO CAPE NEEDED**

"A rare business book that combines tremendous knowledge and insight with an incredibly easy-to-read and approachable style. You'll find yourself turning to it again and again for practical advice on how to communicate better and inspire your workforce."

    - Mark Costa, Chairman and CEO, Eastman Chemical Company

"Simple, smart and fast—that's exactly how this book delivers what leaders need to know to improve performance at their organizations. Strong communication is the lifeblood of effective execution, and David cuts to the chase with insightful, pragmatic roadmaps for leaders."

    - Teresa Paulsen, Vice President, Communication & External Relations, ConAgra Foods

*"What an excellent book for leaders looking for practical tips on how to inspire and motivate a workforce. The challenge in our business world is defining the differences between being a boss and being a leader. **No Cape Needed** sets the vision of what leadership can and should be. This book is a fantastic resource for leaders who really want to move their businesses forward. I highly recommend it."*

    - Dan Costello, President of Home Run Inn Restaurant Group and President of the Chicagoland chapter of the Young Presidents Organization

*"This is an era where the human element in business separates the good from the great. David's **No Cape Needed** shows us how to communicate in a more human way bringing people together and satisfying our innate needs to connect and be heard. This is a book for all people at all levels in any organization."*

    - Shawn Murphy, author, The Optimistic Workplace

"David Grossman taps into his own superpower to clearly and effectively inspire leaders to reach beyond what they know, with actionable suggestions for developing and practicing new ways of communicating. David reminds us that it is not the cape, crown or title that makes a strong leader, but rather trusting, inspiring and empowering others that will lead us to success in communication, leadership and life."

- Jennie P. McConagha, Chief of Staff & Vice President, Operational Communications, MedStar Health

"**No Cape Needed** uses captivating ideas, anecdotes, images, and infographics to give the reader new and deep wisdom about communicating with impact. What a delight to dive into a book about communication and have it be fresh, unique, and compelling—as opposed to the generic stuff that fills so many me-too books about the topic. David Grossman has provided the kind of leadership book that I want to have on my coffee table for me to read again and again as well as in my office waiting room for clients to read—because it is fun, insightful, and every page is filled with enlightening ideas for leaders who want to communicate even more powerfully. To borrow from the Superman metaphor: Look, up in the sky, and everywhere books are sold, it's a leadership communication book that is finally worth reading!"

- Andrew Neitlich, Director, Center for Executive Coaching and co-author, Guerrilla Marketing for a Bulletproof Career

"David Grossman is the caped crusader of workplace communication. And he wants to share his superpower. This gem of a book is full of practical tips and is brilliantly written and designed. David shows you how you too can show up and have the sun shine at your workplace—all through how you communicate. A must read!"

- Dr. Michelle Pizer, Executive Coach, Organisational and Counselling Psychologist

ISBN: 978-1-943277-76-6

Library of Congress Control Number: 2015944275

Printed in the United States of America.
This book is printed on acid-free paper.

Images provided by iStockphoto.com, all rights reserved.

NO CAPE NEEDED

THE SIMPLEST, SMARTEST, FASTEST STEPS TO IMPROVE
HOW YOU COMMUNICATE BY LEAPS AND BOUNDS

by **DAVID GROSSMAN** ABC, APR, Fellow PRSA

"LEADERS BECOME GREAT
NOT BECAUSE OF THEIR POWER,
BUT BECAUSE OF THEIR ABILITY
TO EMPOWER OTHERS."

- JOHN C. MAXWELL

{ FOREWORD

John J. Greisch

CEO, Hill-Rom Holdings, Inc.

David Grossman is a storyteller. This book begins with a reminiscence of his childhood dreams, and similar anecdotes enliven all its pages. This is why we listen to him. This is why we learn from him.

At Hill-Rom, we are fortunate to be in an industry—healthcare—in which there is no shortage of inspiration. Every day, around the world, we enhance outcomes for patients and their caregivers. This is not only our mission, it's our reality. Motivational stories, miraculous stories, humbling stories, heart-warming stories abound. Not just patients, but doctors, nurses, surgeons, and all other manner of caregivers and administrators value our partnership and our products.

Too often, though, our communications focus is on our strategic direction, our financial results, or our operational imperatives, without tying those business mandates to the reason we do what we do. Or we recount stories of patient appreciation, family gratitude, or customer satisfaction, but we do so in such a way that they don't capture the imagination. We serve up these examples, but instead of creating a deep well of inspiration, they evaporate on contact.

Enter David Grossman. Eager to communicate more effectively with our employees, I reached out to him. David's advice? ***"Tell more stories."*** David helped me to focus on the fact that it's not facts and figures that stay with us, it's anecdotes. The more personal and colorful they are, the more powerful they are. Perhaps it's difficult to remember the name and age of a colleague's child, but we certainly remember the time she lost a tooth and wailed:

{ "WHAT IF THE TOOTH FAIRY IS ON VACATION?!"

You can say that patients and caregivers are our passion and watch eyes glaze over.

But if you tell about the service rep who left his family on Christmas Eve to spend the night rounding on the hospital floor, and the egg nog that rep shared with the nurses as Christmas morning dawned, those same eyes light up. You can talk about the importance of innovative solutions—just like the CEO of every other company. Alternatively, you can tell a story about the patient who lost his leg due to nerve damage during a routine procedure, and how that inspired us to create a new kind of surgical positioning equipment that prevents that kind of damage.

With this in mind, I enlisted the help of David and his colleagues to plan a retreat for Hill-Rom's top leaders from around the world. Our company's values and strategy were easy to articulate, but I didn't sense them resonating throughout the organization. I was looking for a way to make these concepts real for our senior leaders, so that the same themes would infuse all their interactions with their own teams. Using many of the same techniques he discusses in this book, David led us through two days of highly interactive, personal exercises. The results were immediate and gratifying. Skeptics became believers, believers became advocates, and all became much more effective communicators. The enthusiasm caused me to schedule a follow-up retreat several months later.

Here is what I learned, with David's guidance:

- Unilateral communication (such as speaking to a large group or sending out group e-mails) is one of the least effective ways to get the audience to receive your message.

- Instead, illustrating your communications with personal anecdotes both humanizes you (making the audience more eager to embrace what you're saying) and makes your message more memorable.

- The more the audience can interact with a concept and make it their own, the more they will truly absorb it and be both moved and equipped to pass it along.

My father also taught me the value of clear and direct communication when I was a teenager. I was working that summer as a landscaper—cutting lawns and trimming bushes and cultivating gardens in the heat of Chicago, where I spent most of my formative years. One day, I came home after a typical 12-hour day in 90-degree temperature and humidity and told my father that I wanted to quit. One of my buddies who was working with me decided that landscaping wasn't for him, and I figured it was time to join him. My dad looked me in the eye and said:

" JOHN, IF YOU WANT TO BE A QUITTER BECAUSE SOMETHING IS TOO HARD, THAT IS YOUR DECISION TO MAKE."

One sentence, one message, one learning—something I have never forgotten and something I have repeated often as a great example of simple, clear and direct communication. The fact that it has shaped me and my work ethic for the last 40 years is a great example of the value of this kind of clear communication, even if it's unpopular.

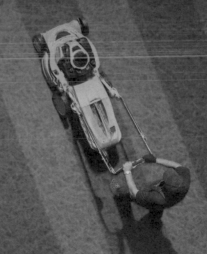

In addition to telling stories to ensure your audience can relate to your message and to you as a communicator, I have learned from David the need to constantly challenge yourself to communicate outside of your comfort zone. I used to intensely dislike public speaking. In high school, I was more like the kid people would never remember as opposed to the loud, brash "leader" most people never forget. As my career progressed, I began to understand the value of communication and the need to be the one out front, regardless of how uncomfortable you may be doing so.

COMMUNICATION IS ALL ABOUT

{ CLARITY,
SIMPLICITY

AND REPETITION OF YOUR MESSAGE.

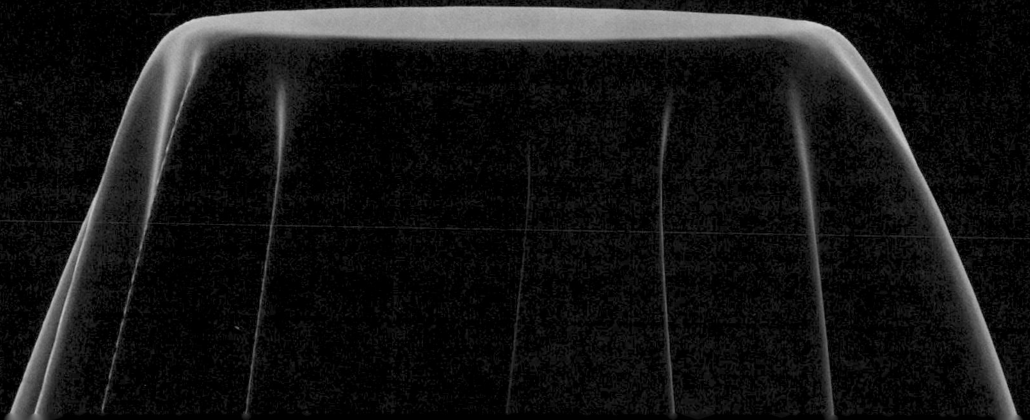

Over the years, I not only learned the value of constant communication, but I have learned to now relish the opportunity to lead by example and to constantly "be on" in front of groups large and small.

The passion with which it is delivered and the ability to personalize your message will enhance your ability to connect with your employees or your audience. Pushing myself out of my comfort zone, while at the same time maintaining my own personal style and credibility, has allowed me to constantly improve my effectiveness as a communicator. David has helped me immensely in this regard. Even after a career spanning 35 years, I have learned there's always a need to become a better communicator.

These learnings are not novel to articulate. However, what distinguishes David Grossman is his ability to help others put them into practice. He has helped me become a more effective leader and CEO by helping me better understand the value of communication. In the pages that follow, David gives the kind of practical advice that has caused us here at Hill-Rom to value his partnership.

He helps make us all a more effective leadership team. ∎

John J. Greisch
CEO, Hill-Rom Holdings, Inc.

CONTENTS

The chapters feature a - - - → list for easy reading and quick reference.

FOREWORD

P. I

PREFACE

P. 21

CHAPTER 1

You Make the Weather

P. 33

CHAPTER 2

Understand Your Audience: Employees

P. 65

CHAPTER 3

Plan for Success

P. 83

CHAPTER 4

Be a Two-Way Communicator

P. 107

ADVICE

The book also includes inspiring leadership tips and advice from CEOs and top leaders.

? WHAT'S THE **BEST** PIECE OF ADVICE YOU'VE RECEIVED IN YOUR CAREER

Make people feel valued and good about themselves and what they do.
P. 43

Laura Nashman
Chief Executive Officer, British Columbia Pension Corporation

Always look for Intersections.
P. 53

Jennifer Leemann
Vice President, Internal Communications, Coach

Lead people, the rest will take care of itself.
P. 59

Rick Phillips
Vice President and Chief Communications Officer, Nationwide

The measure of a leader is less directly tied to their individual accomplishments than it is to the success of the people they lead.
P. 73

Corey duBrowa
SVP, Global Communications, International Public Affairs, Starbucks

Walk a mile in your colleague's shoes.
P. 81

Sherry Vidal-Brown
Executive Vice President, Human Resources, Motel 6

Work harder on yourself than on your job.
P. 87

Skip Prichard
President & CEO, OCLC Leadership Insights blogger at www.skipprichard.com

CHAPTER 5

Cut Through
the Clutter

P. 125

CHAPTER 6

Winning
Presentations

P. 155

CHAPTER 7

Motivate
and Inspire

P. 173

CHAPTER 8

Courageous
Conversations
at Difficult
Times

P. 203

CHAPTER 9

Email
Etiquette
Guide

P. 227

CLOSING
THOUGHT

P. 273

Ask for help before there's a crisis.
P. 101

Anne C. Toulouse
Vice President, Global Brand Management
and Advertising, The Boeing Company

Surround yourself with people greater than you.
P. 105

Carl Chaney
Retired, President and Chief Executive
Officer, Hancock Holding Company

Share mutual respect.
P. 111

Jim Amorosia
CEO, Motel 6

Ask good questions.
P. 119

Mike Fernandez
Corporate Vice President, Cargill

Listen before and more than you talk.
P. 123

Howard N. Karesh
Vice President, Corporate Communications,
Hill-Rom Holdings, Inc.

Define what work-life balance means to you.
P. 133

Mark Yeadon
Senior Vice President of Global Program,
Compassion International

Smile more.
P. 141

Terri Luckett
Chief Financial Officer, Terminal Investments,
Limited S.A

If you always have to be right, there is no space for anyone else in the room.
P. 149

Maribeth Malloy
Director Environmental Sustainability &
External Engagement, Lockheed Martin

Don't let fear dictate decisions.
P. 161

Carolyn M. Rose
Vice President, Talent Effectiveness, Rockwell Automation

Be biased towards action.
P. 171

Duane M. DesParte
Senior Vice President and Corporate Controller, Exelon

Work in an industry that you have a personal passion for.
P. 185

Simon Sproule
Director of Global Marketing and Communications,
Aston Martin

Work is personal.
P. 201

Charlene A. Wheeless
Global Corporate Affairs, Bechtel Corporation

Invest effort into helping people.
P. 211

Mike Henry Sr.
Vice President, Information Technology, SageNet LLC

Never reach a stage in your career where you no longer spend a portion of your time writing.
P. 255

Brett Ludwig
Vice President, Communications, AmerisourceBergen

AS A KID, I LOVED SUPERHEROES.

The famous Justice League of America was a huge hit with me. In fact, I spent way too many hours in front of our television. I'm sure I was sitting within three feet of the TV, hurting my eyes, just so I could turn the channel with ease. Those were the days without remote controls—when you actually needed to get up and change the channel when a show didn't interest you.

For me, it was all about rooting for the superhero. Being the good guy and making a difference were always important to me. ***And I wanted desperately to have my own superpower.***

AS I GREW UP,

the realization settled in—painful as it was—that a superhero's life was not in the cards. Instead, I settled on finding my own heroes, in real life, and learning from them. As I developed in my career as an executive coach and leadership communications strategist working with large corporations, I gravitated to leaders who clearly wanted to use their talents—their "superpowers"—for good, making a real mark on the lives of everyone around them.

I took what I learned from those courageous leaders as the foundation for my business, and have since advised hundreds of Fortune 500 CEOs and leaders at all stages of their careers and countless teams on how to be even more effective.

My message to all my clients is simple:
Communicating effectively gives you tremendous power to transform your company and your team, not to mention your relationships and your life.

Communication really is a way to make a difference. At its simplest, you can use communication to make things easier and more effective and efficient. You also can use communication to make others feel good about their jobs, to be engaged and excited, to help someone who's having a hard time get through a rough patch, or to inspire a team moving through changes or difficult times.

You can use communication for high impact by coaching and mentoring someone, by influencing others who may be tentative or uncomfortable in a new role, or by helping develop a young person to be his or her best self.

In the same way, you can prevent the skeptics and naysayers from spiraling into a negative pattern, or help a struggling individual find the courage and the map to make real change. Lastly, you can use communication to make substantial changes that aren't just about helping a company or team go from "good to great" but instead create a lasting legacy through a new strategic direction.

AND SO MUCH MORE.

That's why I believe that communication is really a superpower in today's world, and certainly in today's business and financial environment.

There's no doubt that some leaders will dismiss communications as a highly critical strategy for success. Some view it as a soft skill, or better left to others, the communications team, or the grapevine. Some view it as a natural talent— you're either a born communicator or you're not—and that informs their willingness to focus on the skill.

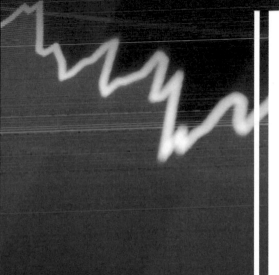

IF EVERYTHING COMMUNICATES,

YOU MIGHT AS WELL DO IT **WELL.**

INTERESTINGLY,

I would tell you this is one skill that's easily accessible, and for a little bit of effort, the payoff can be significant. And for how many things in this world can you get significant results from just a little work?

A lot of people don't think they can communicate well or don't think they can develop the skill. But the truth is that it just takes practice. If leaders at all levels of their organizations come to realize that, great things can happen for their companies. And they can become heroes of their own.

The "Dos" and "Don'ts" I share throughout this book come from work with Fortune 500 clients who are taking the lead globally in the leadership and communication arenas. These aren't just theories; they are proven strategies.

THESE WORK!

I've also asked some of the smartest people I know—leaders in business—to share the best pieces of advice they've received in their careers. You'll see their wisdom peppered throughout the book. I'm grateful to these CEOs and senior executives for allowing the rest of us to learn from what's made them successful.

This book will help you tap the power you have within you to become a courageous, inspirational leader**communicator**™—and do it in your own way. A way that's true to yourself and what's important to you. Let's face it: No superhero cape, magic lasso or flying skills are needed.

JUST YOUR DESIRE, EFFORT AND AN OPENNESS TO CHANGE.

CHAPTER ONE:
You Make The Weather

Hot, Cold, Mild or Stormy? You Decide.

I'm always amazed by how much leaders fail to realize the tremendous influence they have on their team's overall success.

I often boil it down to this: The boss makes the weather.

I used to work for a SVP who was known to be moody. I typically would check with his assistant before meeting with him to determine which way the wind was blowing so I then could adapt my style appropriately. All too often, she told me it was cloudy with a chance of showers. On tornado days, she'd suggest re-scheduling.

In the workplace, how we lead (both what we do and what we say) can prevent weather disasters, and, even better, can create an environment where people do great work and feel terrific about what they're accomplishing. As the song in the musical *Hair* celebrates, we can let the sunshine in.

The employees you lead have a lot to do with the success of your team and your personal success. When engaged and inspired, they can move mountains—driving productivity, business growth, and the success of your organization as a whole.

When employees are disconnected or indifferent, the exact opposite occurs. As a leader of a less-than-inspired team, you might be looking around for someone to blame. But the reality is the buck stops with you. It's up to the leaders to help land on the solutions, then inform, inspire and engage their teams.

Sometimes, we—as leaders—might be rained on, or it might feel like we're getting poured on without an umbrella (and then hung out to dry!). In that case, it's our job to dry off, reflect on what happened, and make great weather for our team as only we can.

In what ways can you make even better weather?

THINK YOU'RE NOT A LEADER.

It's easy to shy away from leadership responsibility by turning to any number of excuses. Someone else above you needs to make the final call. You don't manage people; you're an individual contributor. You're a subject matter expert, not a leader. Your team knows exactly what to do and doesn't need you. You might even simply state: "I'm not the big boss." I hear a lot of "that's not my pay grade." In every case, this type of stance leads to confusion and missteps, large and small.

DO ✓

REALIZE THAT EVERYONE NEEDS TO LEAD.

"Who's in charge here?" It's a phrase many of us have heard in any number of situations and scenarios throughout life—in movies, at work, at home. Yet in successful organizations, being a leader isn't just about people managing others. Instead, it's about helping to make everyone on your team a leader.

Just consider the annual scene of geese flying south for the winter. It's then, when the geese are in search of a warmer climate, that we see the flying-V formation overhead. What's particularly interesting about this is the goose at the apex of the V might be considered the leader. They set the course, lead the way and deal with the most wind in their face.

But that's only for a time. When the lead goose tires, he or she makes its way back to the end of the line and a new goose becomes the leader—setting the course, leading the way, and dealing with the most wind in the face.

In business today, organizations need a similar formation, with everyone leading regardless of whether they manage people or not. And that means everyone needs to be ready to lead when it's their turn.

COMMUNICATION MEANS BUSINESS

Here are some key statistics that demonstrate how better communication improves business results.

EFFECTIVE COMMUNICATION

is **consistently** cited as the

#1

attribute of effective leaders, **according to employees**[1]

79%

of highly engaged employees have **trust** and **confidence** in their leaders[2]

KEY FACTORS BEHIND LEADER EFFECTIVENESS INCLUDE THE LEADER'S ABILITY TO:

Truly understand the factors that **drive business success**	Communicate a **clear and compelling** vision	Inspire employees to **give their best**[3]
62%	61%	55%

Companies with high effectiveness in communication and change management are

3.5 TIMES MORE LIKELY

to **significantly outperform** their less effective peers[4]

Towers Watson has also found that companies with highly effective communicators had

47% HIGHER

total returns to shareholders during the previous five years compared to the least effective communicators[5]

Keeping employees engaged during times of change correlates to an average of

26% HIGHER

productivity rate[6]

Employees who report feeling valued by their employer are

60% MORE LIKELY

to report they are **motivated to do their very best** for their employer[7]

 Highly engaged employees miss fewer days of work and are

THREE TIMES AS LIKELY

as their less-engaged peers to **exceed performance expectations**[8]

THE 4 MAIN PROBLEMS
THAT COME WITH POOR COMMUNICATION

1. A lack of knowing leads to negativity

When people don't have the information or knowledge they feel they need, low productivity results. The reason is pretty basic—people tend to avoid situations in which they will be seen as not knowing, not understanding or not having expertise. No one wants to look like they don't know what to do. And just about everyone has a fear—whether based in reality or not— of being embarrassed or mocked.

Think back to school. From early on through grad school, how many times did you hear teachers and professors say, "There's no such thing as a dumb question?" They knew someone had a question—a very good question that would help shed new light on the conversation—that they were simply too afraid to ask.

2. Employee mistrust, absenteeism and low morale

Employees want to be engaged so they feel connected to the organization. When they are, they are willing to work harder, smarter, and be active in the workplace in ways that drive business results. When they aren't engaged, when they don't feel connected, they suffer. This might seem like a touchy-feely, soft business issue, but unhappy and disconnected employees can have a profound effect on business through absenteeism, lack of motivation, and turnover.

3. Bad interpersonal relationships

How often do you see eyes roll? How much muttering do you quietly hear? When people don't feel connected to each other, it opens up the door for misinterpretation, and for questioning motives and intent. The lack of feeling respected or listened to—truly listened to—leads people to feel negated. When that happens, they often find ways to "push back," even when they can't do it openly or directly.

4. The "Grapevine Effect"

Marvin Gaye isn't the only one who's heard it through the grapevine. No matter how much you might love his Motown hit, you don't want one of these growing in your organization. Yet, by not sharing information, you are ensuring a grapevine will sprout—causing problems and distractions. People want what they can't have, and they naturally assume there is something to be had if they're not shown differently. If you aren't talking proactively about issues that are important to your employees, chances are that someone else is—regardless of the accuracy and truthfulness of their "information."

As the Prince of Soul serenades, "I bet you're wondering how I knew, about your plans to make me blue. It took me by surprise I must say, when I found out yesterday. Don't you know that I heard it through the grapevine…"

Something will be shared by someone, it just won't be what you would say. Perhaps it won't even be correct.

So if there are all these downsides, why aren't we communicating better?

It's not as if management comes to work each day saying, "I want to withhold information." Likewise, employees don't say, "I want to screw something up!" So, what's at play? In many cases, it starts with our beliefs about communication that get in the way. Holding us back from greatness are beliefs and fear.

- We believe we are born good at communicating and therefore don't practice and don't get better
- We're afraid of failing, and that fear stops us from trying and learning new things or skills
- We have a mistaken belief that good communication is all "common sense"
- We inaccurately assume others know what we know

To really address the downsides of poor communication, to get to the many upsides of effective communication and accelerate our business results, we have to examine our beliefs and, in some cases, change them.

Improving communication involves more than just disseminating the message properly so that it's heard (though that alone can be a challenge). It means ensuring that the message resonates with and is understood by the listener(s) in a way that will move them to action. It's hard work, but it's worth it.

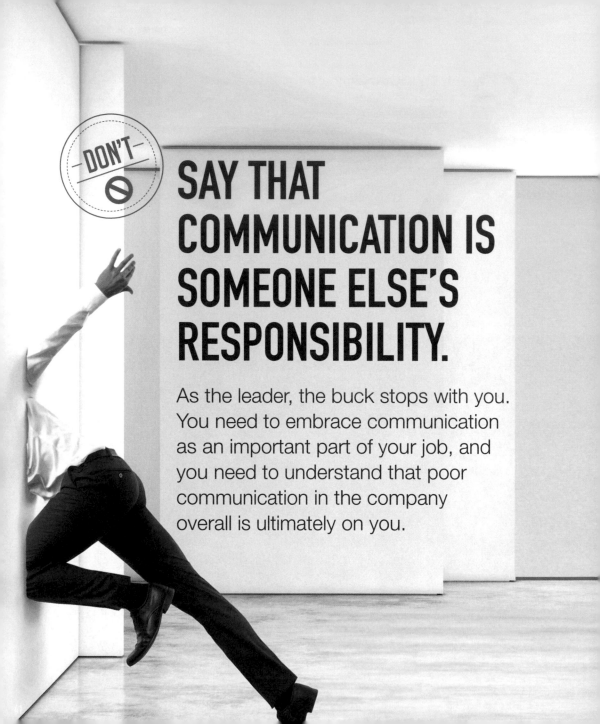

DON'T

SAY THAT COMMUNICATION IS SOMEONE ELSE'S RESPONSIBILITY.

As the leader, the buck stops with you. You need to embrace communication as an important part of your job, and you need to understand that poor communication in the company overall is ultimately on you.

BE ACCOUNTABLE.

Whether it's in your detailed job description or not, leaders at every level of an organization have an important and specific role to connect the dots between the big picture and what it means for employees. No one is more influential than you, the leader.

Specifically, the role of a leader is to:

- Seek out and provide context for organizational information. Your job is to help teams and individuals make sense of what they read and hear

- Make information relevant so every employee knows how he or she fits in, and the valued role each has

- Provide job-related information so your team receives essential information that helps them do their jobs even more effectively and efficiently

- Provide information and inspiration, which could include feedback on individual performance, recognition of achievements, celebration, and so on

Many leaders underestimate the power they have, and empowerment they can provide by how they lead and the accountability they take.

 A boss creates fear, a leader confidence. A boss fixes blame, a leader corrects mistakes. A boss knows all, a leader asks questions. A boss creates fire, a leader creates passion.

– Russell H. Ewing, British Journalist

WHAT'S THE BEST PIECE OF ADVICE YOU'VE RECEIVED IN YOUR CAREER

Advice:
Make people feel valued and good about themselves and what they do.

Back Story: We all thrive when we feel confident, competent and valued. When what we do is acknowledged. When we are recognized for the contribution made. When our humanity is respected, and we are welcomed and embraced for who we are and what we uniquely bring to the table. And when dignity is above all the most valued purpose.

As a leader, your voice is powerful—it has the power to ignite and engage people in the most positive and productive ways. Our power as leaders can also erode confidence in others, leaving them feeling empty, lost and demotivated. Recognize the power you wield and use it for good.

Outcome: This requires that you start from a position of trust. You believe the people around you are working hard, trying their best and wanting to contribute to the success of your company. (Where this is not true, you have other problems). Everything flows from trust.

And even when it doesn't work out, where tough decisions need to be made that will negatively affect your people, you must execute those decisions while maintaining people's dignity. You will know you have achieved this when someone thanks you after being let go from their job. Even in this most trying circumstance, dignity must prevail. I had the privilege to see this in action learning from a leader who had people's dignity top of mind. It was a lesson in what's really important, learned very early on for me— and a lesson I am grateful for and try every day to live by.

Laura Nashman
Chief Executive Officer,
British Columbia Pension
Corporation

DON'T JUST LEAD OTHERS.

One's not a leader without followers; yet to be effective, the focus can't be just on those who follow.

Leadership involves persuading other people to follow and set aside their individual concerns for at least a brief time to pursue a common goal.

DO START BY LEADING YOURSELF.

Get to know yourself better.

The choices you make are a direct result of how you're wired and what makes you tick. Ensure you understand your motivations, along with being in touch with your inner state. Understanding what's happening with you emotionally will allow you to respond thoughtfully instead of react. Understand, recognize and appreciate the inner complexity that's you. That's how you can awaken the leader within.

DON'T
⊘SPEED THROUGH YOUR COMMUNICATIONS.

Real conversations are becoming extinct in many organizations today.

We take 30 minutes to write five confusing back-and-forth emails but won't take three minutes to pick up the phone for a simple conversation. Don't fall into this trap.

DO
✓TAKE TIME TO CREATE UNDERSTANDING.

Move over technology, and make room for meaning.

Learn to recognize real two-way communication and what it takes. No cheap alternatives accepted. The truisms about two-way communication:

- Effective communication is a conversation
- The goal is shared understanding and meaning
- Shared meaning is often assumed but should be confirmed
- Training and skill building improves your communication effectiveness
- Active listening is a critical skill, because it helps derive meaning

-DON'T-

🚫

DICTATE.

47

Increasingly, great leaders recognize that transformative leadership isn't about telling people what to do. Instead, it's about equipping and then empowering teams to make smart decisions together, respecting the collective brainpower of the group. Great leadership is never about dictating your own vision and way of doing things. Leaders with a "my way or the highway" mentality won't connect with their teams.

48

ENGAGE OTHERS TO PARTICIPATE IN DECISION-MAKING.

As a leader, how do you get people to follow? One of the most important things is helping employees feel that they're significant, that they matter. Employees want to feel a sense of purpose around their work, that they're part of something larger than they are.

And of course, employees want the sense of excitement that comes only from knowing that they're truly contributing to the success of the company. One of the best ways to involve employees is to ensure you're asking them the tough questions, such as: What can change here? What could be different? What might we consider doing different or getting rid of?

One of the CEOs I work with frequently visits manufacturing sites and plants. When he does, he always asks this pointed question: "What's something really stupid that we're doing that we could or should stop doing?"

It's amazing how many insightful ideas and perspectives he gets from that question, simply because he takes the time to ask and is sincere with his request.

When you involve employees in decision-making, you boost morale and productivity and increase employee satisfaction. In many cases, you also build greater customer satisfaction and can more easily cut unnecessary costs. Plus, when employees are involved in solving a business challenge, they're more likely to accept the solution—whatever it may be—because they have ownership in the outcome.

FOSTER INNOVATION
BY EMPOWERING YOUR TEAMS

Recent research published in the *Harvard Business Review*[9] on the timely topic of fostering innovation within companies underscores the value of encouraging employees to be decision-makers. The researchers, led by Harvard business scholar Linda Hill and former Pixar technology guru Greg Brandeau, spent hundreds of hours studying industries as wide ranging as filmmaking, e-commerce, auto manufacturing, professional services, high tech and luxury goods. They found that the most successful innovation leaders focused heavily on collaborative team building.

"They (the innovative leaders) didn't see themselves as setting a direction and then leading the charge," the researchers wrote in HBR. "…They knew they could not be 'chief innovator' or the driver of innovation who proactively 'made it happen.' They had learned that casting themselves as a 'Follow me!' leader was far less likely to produce the collective genius.

"Instead, they consistently saw their role as that of creating a context or setting—it could range from a team to an entire firm—where people are willing and able to do the hard work innovative problem-solving requires. As one of them told us, 'My job is to set the stage, not to perform on it.'" This insight shows that collaboration is not just a nice-to-have. It's essential to any progressive company's long-term success.

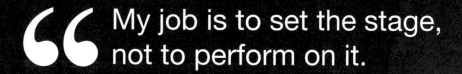

" My job is to set the stage, not to perform on it.

TOUGH DECISIONS MADE EASIER WITH EMPLOYEE INPUT

You want to know if your audience:	Ask them:
Heard your key messages or if they need more context or detail	*"What are your key takeaways from the information I just shared?"*
Understood the "why" and the "what" behind a change initiative	*"What challenges and opportunities do you see with what I've just explained?"*
Is comfortable with the messages you're communicating or if they have feedback	*"What's your reaction to what I've just shared with you?"*
Has any other questions	*"What other questions do you have?"*

WHAT'S THE
BEST
PIECE OF ADVICE
YOU'VE RECEIVED
IN YOUR CAREER

Advice:
Always look for Intersections.

Back Story: Early in my career I thought I needed to know everything about one topic, but I was given the advice to always know at least two disciplines. I've often encountered individuals who are afraid to step outside of their focus area, but in today's fast-paced environment the newest ideas sit at the intersections of unrelated fields.

Outcome: By constantly learning about different areas, you'll be inspired with unexpected ways to solve problems. It enables you to discover bigger trends and create innovation in unexpected places. It also helps you see patterns that might not emerge if you focus too narrowly.

Jennifer Leemann
Vice President,
Internal Communications,
Coach

DON'T

SHUT OUT ENGAGEMENT ON A PERSONAL LEVEL.

It's a common misperception that great leaders rarely reveal their humanity. I often say that leaders who are aloof with their teams are committing the "sin of detachment." Most influential leaders understand that connecting on a personal level with employees is critical to their success.

DO ✓

LEARN ABOUT YOUR EMPLOYEES' LIVES.

If you're guilty of detachment, ask yourself how well you know your team. What are they passionate about? What are the little things that matter to them? When was the last time you interacted with them as people, not simply as your employees? When was the last time you said, "Thank you?"

By engaging with team members and employees, leaders can boost morale, engagement and excitement. Studies have shown that motivated and involved teams are measurably more productive and successful than disengaged teams. People won't listen to you until they know who you are and that you care.

56

DON'T 🚫

TRY TO BE SOMEONE ELSE.

It can be tempting at times to adopt a leadership style that you appreciate in a boss.

Want to be that amazing motivational leader who delivers killer presentations at the sales conference? Or the CEO with a knack for sizing up the numbers in a moment's notice? Or how about that executive with the classic, outgoing style that has everyone circling around him or her? All those personality traits can be assets, but you'll waste a lot of time if that's not you, and your team won't respond if they know you're not being authentic.

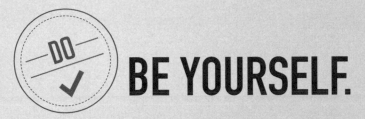

BE YOURSELF.

Remember that you don't have to be the most vocal person in the room to command respect. Instead, be yourself and know your leadership style. Understanding yourself can help you maximize your effectiveness, while staying true to your values and approach. A goal to strive for is to show up more as who you are in the workplace.

Which are more effective communicators?

EXTROVERTS *or* INTROVERTS?

And the award goes to…both. Each style can be highly effective, if you manage the typical downsides. Here's what we know:

- **Introverts** think they're communicating more than they actually are. However, the quality of their communications are high

- **Extroverts** are the opposite. They communicate frequently, but the quality of their communications are typically low

Introverts, take notice and increase the frequency of your communications. Extroverts, work to improve the quality of what you communicate.

Either way, that's style-ish advice for any leader.

? | WHAT'S THE BEST PIECE OF ADVICE YOU'VE RECEIVED IN YOUR CAREER

Advice:
Lead people, the rest will take care of itself.

Back Story: Many years ago, when I became a new leader, I was impressed by the sheer volume of things I was managing. There were complicated projects, important committees, and understanding budgets for the first time. It was very overwhelming for a first-time leader. I remember discussing it with a mentor of mine. He gently reminded me that, "You're not here to lead 'things.' You're here to lead people. If you remember that, all the projects, budgets and activity will take care of itself."

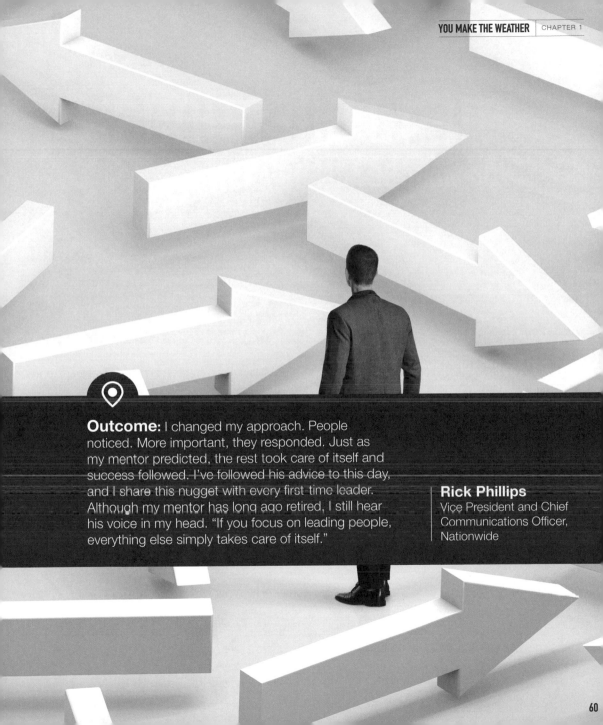

Outcome: I changed my approach. People noticed. More important, they responded. Just as my mentor predicted, the rest took care of itself and success followed. I've followed his advice to this day, and I share this nugget with every first-time leader. Although my mentor has long ago retired, I still hear his voice in my head. "If you focus on leading people, everything else simply takes care of itself."

Rick Phillips
Vice President and Chief
Communications Officer,
Nationwide

THE 13 QUESTIONS
YOU MUST BE ABLE TO ANSWER

Employees want a leader who is real and is aware (and honest about) his or her strengths and weaknesses. They don't want a leader who's like a Hollywood movie set—well-packaged on the outside with nothing behind it. Inspiring employees and engaging them is about meeting their strategic communication needs. Here are the most common questions employees have for their leaders, which should form the basis of a leader's set of core messages and actions.

1. How did you get to where you are?

2. How do you want people to know you?
    What makes you tick?

3. What are your expectations of employees?

4. What should employees expect of you?

5. On what do you want to put a stake in the ground?

6. What's your vision? Why should various audiences believe in you and the vision?

7. Who are we and what do we do?

8. What are our business goals? Business strategies?

9. What initiatives will drive the business today? In the future?

10. What are the new behaviors you expect employees to perform successfully to achieve your results? How will we get the results needed?

11. What does success look like?

12. How will we measure success?

13. What needs to change to make this happen?

SABOTAGE OTHERS' TRUST IN YOU.

As leaders, we can't underestimate the power of the shadow we cast and, subsequently, our ability to influence behaviors to drive results. We shouldn't just talk about the business strategy; we have to demonstrate visibly what it looks like.

—DO—
✓

DEMONSTRATE THAT YOU CAN BE TRUSTED.

As a leader, trust starts—or stops—with you. Trust is contagious. When you trust others and demonstrate that you can be trusted, it builds an opportunity for others to trust and be worthy of trust. By contrast, if you distrust, then others will too.

Here are a few of the ways to build trust in everyday scenarios:

- Keep your promises—whether seemingly significant or small—and others will, too
- Give credit when others do great work. Employees will appreciate it and follow suit
- Admit that things went wrong or didn't turn out as you had planned. Employees will see you as accountable, credible and focused on being better, and they'll follow your lead
- Be approachable and friendly. People trust leaders they like
- Balance the need for results with being considerate of others and their feelings
- Instead of using your position power, work hard to win over people
- Ensure your words and your actions match
- Actively listen and check for understanding by paraphrasing what you've heard
- Show support for your team members, even when mistakes are made
- Be honest and tell the truth: Telling people what you think they want to hear erodes trust
- Collaborate with others across teams and functions and avoid silos and turf battles, signaling to your team to do the same. Work will get done better and faster, not to mention more peacefully

Trust Means:

- Deserving confidence
- Being dependable
- Being reliable
- Doing what you say you will do

CHAPTER TWO: Know Your Audience: Employees

What Every Employee Wants

To truly move employees to action, we have to know what they care about and get into their mindset. In a nutshell, here's their short list:

Less BS and more humanity. Enough beating around the bush or, worse yet, "spinning" of messages. Employees want to know what's happening and why in a direct way. Tell me what you know when you know it. Chances are, you're waiting too long after getting key information to communicate it.

Understanding your expectations. People rise to the expectations set for them. Many problems in business are caused by a lack of understanding of expectations or a misunderstanding of what's needed and expected.

More listening. Stop talking so much. Ask for input and feedback. People are more likely to support what they help create. Stop the monologues and talking at your employees; let's have real, two-way conversations.

Take action on employee suggestions. The action might be as simple as looping back with the employee to share appreciation for their thoughts, and help them understand why you're not implementing their suggestion for an alternative approach. In this way, you're closing the feedback loop, which can be as worthwhile as implementing an employee's suggestion.

Show employees you care (in a genuine way). Find out what's important to employees, and please be sure to acknowledge critical milestones that are important to them.

Empathize with your teams. Pause and imagine how employees truly feel. Show you hear them, and validate their feelings. The payoff is an employee who knows you care; at the same time, you gather information that's useful to motivating that employee.

Recognize and appreciate employees. Say "thank you" for a job well done. Reinforce very specifically the behaviors you want to continue seeing.

Which of these strategies would have the greatest positive impact on your employees?

DON'T

ASSUME
YOU KNOW
WHAT YOUR
EMPLOYEES
NEED.

As leaders, we spend much of our time and effort setting business goals and developing plans to achieve them. Yet the most important element behind everything is your team. If they don't understand where they fit in, all of our lofty goals will go nowhere.

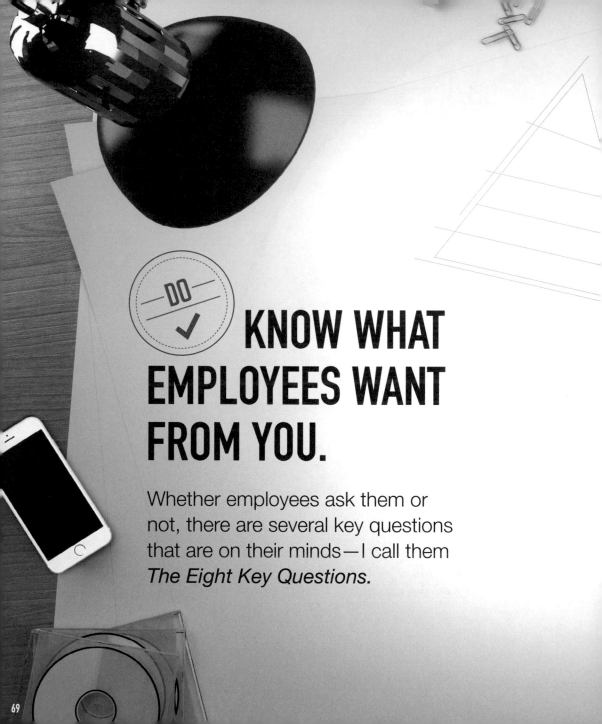

DO ✓ KNOW WHAT EMPLOYEES WANT FROM YOU.

Whether employees ask them or not, there are several key questions that are on their minds—I call them *The Eight Key Questions.*

These questions are a lot like Maslow's Hierarchy of Needs, which states that only after a person has fulfilled certain levels of needs can he or she begin to move to more complex levels of thought, such as self-awareness and understanding of others. In other words, employees' basic needs—the "me-focused" needs—have to be addressed first before employees can begin to think beyond themselves.

Once employees feel taken care of, they become more aware of changes or initiatives happening outside their department or function and ask the question, "What's going on?" This is a transitional question that takes employees from "me" to "we." The "we-focused" questions that follow are really about the larger organization.

The ultimate payoff is when employees ask "How can I help?" This is an expression of engagement—a willingness to do more—which also demonstrates a strong emotional connection to the organization.

It's important to remember that these are questions that employees think about, and perhaps ask, every day—whether they are new to the organization or veterans. When change happens, employees immediately go back to the me-focused questions. Our job as leaders is to get them back to question number eight as quickly as possible ("How can I help?"). If we don't, that's when business often gets stopped, slowed, or interrupted, as employees work through—or are challenged by—change.

The 8 Key Questions™

8. How can I help?
7. What's our vision and values?
6. How are we doing? — **WE**
5. What's our business strategy?
4. What's going on? — **TRANSITION**
3. Does anyone care about me?
2. How am I doing? — **ME**
1. What's my job?

DON'T
🚫 **BUY IN TO AN EMPLOYEE'S DESIRE TO KNOW SOMETHING ABOUT EVERYTHING THAT'S GOING ON IN YOUR ORGANIZATION.**

It's impossible to accomplish and is also an unrealistic expectation.

DO
✓ **FOCUS ON MISSION-CRITICAL INFORMATION, AND SHARE THOSE EXPECTATIONS WITH EMPLOYEES.**

Follow these two guidelines for when to share (or not share) information:

1. A leader's top priority is sharing information employees need to do their jobs well (work- or job-focused information designed to help employees perform their best)
2. A secondary priority is sharing information so employees can advocate on behalf of the organization as brand ambassadors (typically information that builds pride and morale or is important to help get out the organization's story)

Sharing these expectations with staff is critical so they know what to expect from you. One other key expectation to share with employees: If they don't know something or have questions, they need to seek out the information. Communicating is not a spectator sport—it requires active participation.

5 SIMPLE

YET POWERFUL STEPS TO SHOW YOUR EMPLOYEES YOU CARE ABOUT THEM:

- **Find out and remember what they are passionate about:** How would they spend a Saturday? At a museum? A concert? Do they golf? Do they have a favorite sports team?

- **Demonstrate you know the little things that matter to them:** Do they have a TV show they watch regularly? What might be on their minds as they come to work?

- **Remember their birthdays:** Consider putting these dates in your calendar as a reminder.

- **Interact with them as people, not just your employees:** Say hi. Ask them how their weekend went—and demonstrate active listening.

- **Say thank you and share specific appreciative feedback.**

WHAT'S THE
BEST
PIECE OF ADVICE
YOU'VE RECEIVED
IN YOUR CAREER

Advice:
Remember that the measure of a leader is less directly tied to their individual accomplishments than it is to the success of the people they lead.

Back Story: My first—and best—encounter with leadership was in the person of Willis "Bill" Winter, a professor I came to admire at the University of Oregon while studying in the school of Journalism. Bill was one of those lovably gruff fellows from the old school whose demeanor was pitched somewhere between Jackie Gleason and Jimmy Stewart: part wise guy and part wise man.

Bill was seldom in his office—a more common place to run into him would have been the classroom, or a public space on campus where he'd be surrounded by a crowd of current and former students biding their time for just a moment of his wisdom—but when he was, cigarette smoke would be wafting out from behind a door papered over with what he called "Bingo Board Material," a.k.a. notes from former U of O students letting him know that they'd landed a job in advertising somewhere in the wider world beyond Allen Hall, upon which he would scribble "BINGO" in dark black Sharpie.

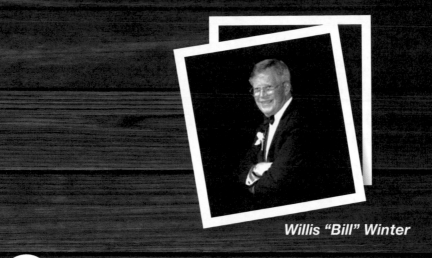

Willis "Bill" Winter

Outcome: Bill is the guy who taught me how to shake someone's hand properly — "not too strong, but definitely not too soft, and you need to make sure the web between your thumb and index finger ***really gets in there***" (grabbing my hand abruptly to ingrain his point in my memory) — and how to write a professional thank you note that would not only graciously convey gratitude upon the recipient, but place someone front and center in their memory when it came time to make a hiring decision.

But the biggest leadership lesson that Bill taught wasn't any one phrase, or thing, or behavior — it was that the measure of a leader is less directly tied to their individual accomplishments than it is to the success of the people they coach, mentor, teach and shape into future leaders. Later in life, I would go on to serve on the University of Oregon's Alumni Association Board and the Journalism School's Advisory Council, and the sole reason for both of these investments of time and energy can be laid at the feet of one of the most inspiring, thoughtful people with whom I've ever had the pleasure of an extended debate. If I am any kind of leader at all, it is because I was busy paying attention to what a terrific man Bill Winter was, every minute I was around him. He was an ad guy who let the life he led be his best advertisement.

Corey duBrowa
SVP, Global
Communications,
International Public
Affairs, Starbucks

ASSUME EMPLOYEES KNOW HOW THEY CONTRIBUTE.

Too often, leaders assume employees fully understand their role and how their work contributes to the company's overall success. Yet if you ask the average employee, they often can't answer those critical questions. They truly don't know how they fit in and why they matter.

DO ✓

CLARIFY EACH EMPLOYEE'S ROLE

Leaders at every level of an organization have an important and specific role to help employees connect the dots between the big business picture and what it means for them.

When employees understand their role, they can articulate it and say how they are helping drive business results. Their role can be articulated as what they do, or even better, how they contribute. There's an often-told story about two bricklayers. You ask one what he's doing and he says, "I'm building a wall." You ask the other what he's doing and he says, "I'm building a castle."

Organizations need people who build walls. More importantly, they desperately need employees who are castle builders. Which are your employees? The only way to know is to ask, and to coach if you're needing to widen their view on how they contribute to the overall strategy.

Tie All Your Communications To An Element Of The Strategy:

All your communications should explicitly link to an element of the strategy so employees understand how what they do connects. This also reinforces the importance of the strategy.

- **Reviewing an agenda for the next senior leadership meeting?** How does it explicitly reinforce the strategy and goals? Too many agendas are updates on what's been accomplished by departments or regions instead of updates as they relate to critical areas of the strategy.

- **Want to recognize someone for their results?** As you share appreciative feedback, make sure to connect the results back to one of your core values and behaviors.

- **Sharing a business update at an all-employee meeting?** Use the strategy as an organizing factor for your remarks, and mention explicitly each of the core components of the strategy.

DON'T 🚫 THINK YOU'RE THE SMARTEST AND MOST INTERESTING PERSON IN THE ROOM.

Leaders all too often suffer from "most interesting person in the room" syndrome. That means they can sometimes talk without saying much, or assume that because they're talking, everyone is hearing the message in exactly the way it is intended.

DO ✔ INVITE YOUR EMPLOYEES TO CONTRIBUTE SUBSTANTIALLY TO THE CONVERSATION.

Communication is far more than talking, emailing, sending out the occasional memo, or whatever your version is of getting the word out. In fact, good communication should be planned, consistent, and *always take into account employee needs and concerns.*

Good communication isn't about talking at your listeners; it's about engaging them in order to gain their perspective, along with their respect, interest, and attention. You want people to feel that you are talking with them, and empathizing with their concerns and situation.

TIPS FOR BUILDING EMPLOYEE ENGAGEMENT

THE POWER OF
DELEGATING

Have you ever found yourself saying, "it's just easier to do it myself?" or "Why do I bother, it isn't going to be done like I want it to be done?" Often when you find yourself saying these types of phrases, you and your communication—or lack thereof—are the ones to blame or look at first. Very often we don't delegate well because we don't take the time to clearly communicate our expectations.

This is such a great example of the myth "I don't have time to communicate." You do when you realize that the time you spend communicating will keep problems from happening and will usually reward you by creating more time long-term.

THE GROWING INFLUENCE OF
AMBASSADORS

Increasingly, companies are seeing great results from engaging employee "ambassadors" on their teams. Whether the ambassadors are part of a formal group or simply tapped as some of your most vocal company supporters, find ways to engage them! Especially during times of change, these ambassadors can work on the front lines to generate buy in for the company's new direction. Building that team of ambassadors over time can be an especially wise way of creating a wide base of employee fans to outspokenly defend and support the company's long-term vision and goals. In many ways, they can serve as a natural extension of your employee communications team. They can also be extended eyes and ears to help you keep a pulse on what's real in the business.

–DON'T–

IGNORE THE FULL POTENTIAL OF THE PERFORMANCE REVIEW.

If the annual performance review is a check-off-the-box activity, you're missing a key opportunity to engage and motivate your employees.

DO ✓

MAKE THE PERFORMANCE REVIEW A CHANCE TO INSPIRE.

I was talking with a client recently who was planning for her face-to-face performance review meetings with her staff. With forms completed, she acknowledged she didn't want to simply review the content of the forms.

Instead, her intention was to have the most productive and positive dialogue possible. That meant she needed to ask a lot of questions, plus respond. We discussed what some important questions might be where she'd gain valuable information and her staff would feel valued and appreciated.

Here were a few of the questions we discussed:

- What needs to happen to make this meeting highly motivating for you?
- Can you summarize how you did at meeting your performance objectives?
- Your greatest successes?
- Your biggest challenges?
- What problems, suggestions for changes or improvements do you have?
- What have I done to help or hinder your performance?
- What can I do to help you improve?
- What do you want most from your job?
- Is your ultimate career objective the same or has it changed since our last discussion?

- What would you like your next position to be? How do you think you can best work toward that goal?
- Wrap up: Can you summarize the greatest strengths and what you should keep doing? Similarly, the issues you need to work on?
- Follow-up. How can I best support you? What can I do more of, the same amount of, or less of for you?
- What's the best way we can monitor performance on this/these issue(s)?

WHAT'S THE **BEST** PIECE OF ADVICE YOU'VE RECEIVED IN YOUR CAREER ?

Advice:
Walk a mile in your colleague's shoes (show empathy).

Back Story: In a large organization like ours, getting people to understand the important part that each function plays in the success of the whole operation is critical. That's why I feel it's so important to create opportunities for people to be exposed to other departments through cross-functional projects.

Outcome: When we've done that, I've seen people have such greater empathy and understanding for other functions' roles. In that way, they've learned how to truly create change and achieve the company's overall goals for the business.

Sherry Vidal-Brown
Executive Vice President,
Human Resources,
Motel 6

CHAPTER THREE: Plan For Success

Communicating, Like It Or Not.

As I often say, "You can't NOT communicate," but leaders often figure they can avoid communicating with their teams and just focus on the "important work." Here's what leaders don't realize: They are already communicating whether or not they intend to. It is human nature for others to read into our actions based on their perceptions. And as we know, actions speak louder than words.

A recent experience I had cooking with a friend brings home this message.

I love to cook, and I'm a clean-as-you-go kind of cook. A friend of mine had a different approach, something that I didn't realize until she visited my home.

At the end of the meal preparation, just as we were about to sit down for dinner, guess what happened? There were dirty dishes everywhere. The sink was piled so high that I thought it would topple over. I tried to take a deep breath and tell myself, 'David, now's the time to flex your style. This will be good for you.' But that didn't work. We sat down for the meal and the food just didn't taste as good to me. Why? Because I knew what my kitchen looked like. I just couldn't enjoy myself.

Isn't communications just like that? Isn't it amazing that we always can find the time to clean up the messes? The truth is we can always find time in a crisis. So, why is it that we can't find time to plan and be purposeful in the quieter moments?

That's one of the most important learnings here. Communicating well should actually save you time and energy. It should help you move through change faster, and it will definitely accelerate the path to your goals. As for a stress-free cooking and dining experience, well that just depends on how organized your cooking partner wants to be.

How can you be even more purposeful knowing you can't NOT communicate?

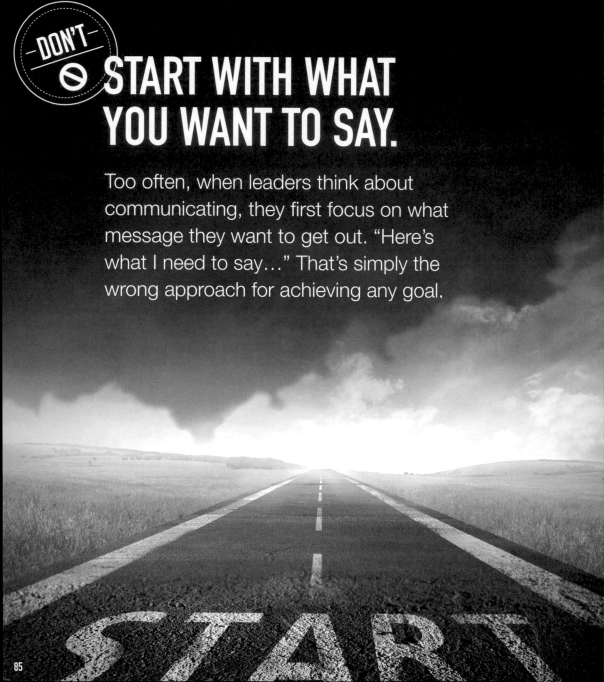

DON'T START WITH WHAT YOU WANT TO SAY.

Too often, when leaders think about communicating, they first focus on what message they want to get out. "Here's what I need to say…" That's simply the wrong approach for achieving any goal.

START WITH THE BUSINESS OUTCOME YOU SEEK.

Instead of thinking about the message or the vehicle, focus on the business impact you want to have.

We spend a fair amount of time talking with our clients and the leaders we work with about "desired outcomes"—the first step in planning any kind of communication.

When we ask, "What's the outcome you seek?" we often get a communications goal. (For example, I want to send an email.) That's helpful to know but communications should never be an outcome; it's a means to achieving a business outcome. When we follow up: "What's the business outcome you seek?" we often get puzzled looks from some.

That's why I believe it's so important to understand what we mean by outcome, given its importance. The better we can define what we need to accomplish, the better the chance we will succeed at achieving it. After all, if we don't know where we're going, how will we get there?"

An outcome is an observable end result, a consequence, a change in business performance, something that follows from an action.

When we ask about a desired outcome, we want a business objective. That is, a measurable result like growth in the organization, productivity gains, faster time to market, customers served, share of market, or people in seats. This kind of outcome is a consequence of work by teams and individuals whose goal is to deliver on the business objective.

Another way to look at this: If what you want to communicate isn't about moving the business forward, it's important to think long and hard about whether you should be communicating at all.

WHAT'S THE
BEST
PIECE OF ADVICE
YOU'VE RECEIVED
IN YOUR CAREER

Advice:
Work harder on yourself than on your job.

Back Story: Thinking that hard work was the key to success, I was surprised the first time I heard Jim Rohn share this success tip. And that started me on the lifelong quest of personal development. If you work hard on you, you grow your capacity, your output, and your influence. The bonus was that when I stopped working on a task and instead focused on learning a skill, I found the work more enjoyable. When you enjoy your work, you perform better. That cycle perpetuates and helps create success.

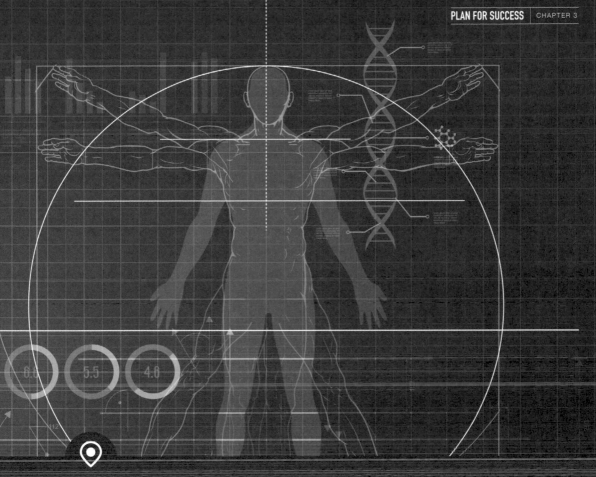

Outcome: As a CEO, I often surprise employees by giving them this advice instead of focusing on a short-term goal. The same principle that worked to make me effective and fueled my professional success works for everyone. If all of us in the organization are working on ourselves, we end up with a stronger organization all dedicated to serving others. I've led several companies and dramatic financial turnarounds, and this tip is always a part of the success.

Skip Prichard
President & CEO, OCLC
Leadership Insights blogger
at www.skipprichard.com

DON'T ⊘ JUST WING IT.

Too often, when it comes to communication, things are thrown together at the last minute. It's an afterthought. Or, worse yet, there's an overconfidence that "we've got it." Yet when you wing it, it also becomes more difficult to handle objections and tough situations. And, it becomes a lot harder to clean up.

DO ✓

PLAN

Often leaders assume that as long as they have ideas, a vision, and a sense of purpose, that will be enough to lead the way forward. If only it were that easy. In truth, good leaders know the importance of planning and clearly spelling out the path ahead.

You need to have a plan for communicating your vision, painting a picture of it, and helping people understand how it will affect them.

take 5™ To Communicate Well

Being more purposeful in your communications can take as little as five minutes. I call it "take 5" to communicate well. The process involves following five simple steps that can lead to better communication. With time, leaders can get so good at answering these questions that they can work through this on the back of a napkin. Most importantly, the messages they eventually deliver to their audiences will be better thought out and tied to the business outcomes they seek.

Remember, messages will best resonate with your audiences if you first think about where the audience is coming from and the audience's current mindset. Well–thought-out messages are also more likely to move your audience to action.

The take 5 steps in a nutshell:

1. **Outcome.** What do you want to accomplish at the highest level? What's the business outcome you seek? Define it as specifically as you can.

2. **Audience.** Who's the audience? Where are they coming from? What do you want them to think, feel, and do?

3. **Messages.** Given the key audiences' mindset, what are the two or three messages to move them to action?

4. **Tactics.** Is the message best delivered face-to-face, one-on-one, through email, or in another way? Consider the limitations and possible impact of each option. Important and sensitive topics deserve face-to-face communication, or at least voice-to-voice communication

5. **Measurement.** How will you know when you're successful? How do you evaluate how well your message is being received? Body language or verbal response? Other feedback mechanisms? One way is to analyze the questions employees ask. If they are forward looking and asking how a new situation might work, your message is getting through. If they are challenging your assumptions or want to take a step back, you could do a better job communicating.

HOW MUCH TIME DO YOU SPEND
COMMUNICATING?

We've established that leaders are always communicating—even when they don't realize they are. It's fair to say that 80 to 90 percent of the average leader's week is spent communicating. Yet, how much time are those same leaders spending on planning for those communications, and thinking about the messages that they send? That's more like 10 percent.

It's a fact that leaders are used to putting time and energy into business plans, product launches, business succession plans, and more, but when it comes to planning for day-to-day communications, most fall down on the job. As I like to say, the Nike slogan, "Just Do it!" doesn't apply here. You can wing it and take a chance on your results, or you can make a plan and significantly increase your impact.

INFORMATION DOES NOT
= COMMUNICATION

Information and communication are not the same. Information is just words; communication is about moving people to action. There are four components that distinguish communication from information. In order to truly communicate, you must:

- **Understand your audience:** Adjust your message to best match your audience. Communicate to them, not just to anyone. You also shouldn't just share data; you need to shape information in a way that has meaning for a particular audience. Think of it as the difference between a bookkeeper printing out financial reports for you, and a controller or CFO interpreting the data into critical information that is important to help you understand or make decisions.

- **Engage your audience:** Involve them to get their respect, interest and attention—not to mention great ideas. Ask questions and use empathy to convey sincerity.

- **Be truthful and direct:** You must have respect for people so that they will reciprocate that respect and buy in to your communications.

- **Plan your method for communicating:** Email is not the best way to communicate. Face to face, in person, "live"—whatever you want to call it, this is best when communication is about a tough issue or is a tough message. And, remember, there's no winging it—every communication, even those that are in person, needs to be strategic, prepared for and planned.

COMMUNICATE FROM YOUR PERSPECTIVE.

-DON'T-

Sure, it makes sense that you would approach any message from your point of view. It's human nature to assume that others share your perspective and will perceive topics the same way you do.

Yet over the course of my career, many leaders have lamented this: "Little I say seems to be resonating!" Although this can be very frustrating, it certainly does not mean that you should just stop communicating (as I've also heard…).

Most likely, the failure to communicate effectively is an indicator that you're communicating from your perspective, and you haven't taken the time to find out what makes your audience tick, and how and when they're most receptive to information.

66 **We're very clear in our own heads about what we think.**

UNDERSTAND YOUR AUDIENCE'S PERSPECTIVE.

I heard an interesting comparison recently. When you see people on the street talking to themselves, they are often labeled as "insane." Yet what do we call it when we talk to ourselves inside organizations? "Marketing or communications." Leaders do this kind of thing—speak from their own perspectives—far too often. Instead, they need to look at every interaction with employees as a precious chance to meet them where they are.

The more you know about someone, the better you're able to persuade them and move them to action. There's real magic in addressing your audience's needs first. When you do, your audience is more likely to trust you, and as a result, be more generous, open and receptive to big-picture, strategic communication.

Remember:
Think, Feel, Do

Get Inside Your Audience's Head

To understand where your audience is coming from, here are some key questions to consider:

- What is the audience's special perspective on my topic?
- What do they already know?
- What are their positive or negative perceptions?
- What are they concerned about?

Communication at its finest is about shared understanding and moving people to action. Beyond understanding someone's mindset, we need to be clear about what we want our audience to do. There's a process people go through before they act. We think. Then, we feel.

Once we know what the action is that we seek, we can plan for what we want our audience to think and feel and how to drive that action. And it forces us to think about the situation from the audience's perspective.

THINK: What one or two things do we want our audience to think?

FEEL: What one or two things do we want our audience to feel?

DO: What do we want our audience to do as a result of our communication?

DON'T JUST SAY SOMETHING IMPORTANT ONCE.

It's crucial to look at your communications as a process of repetition. Too often, leaders think of communication as a "check-off-the-box" activity. For example, they'll think, "I sent an email. Therefore, I communicated." By doing so, they confuse getting the message out with actually creating shared meaning and understanding.

DO ✓ FOLLOW UP WITH MATERIALS TO HELP YOUR AUDIENCE RETAIN AND PROCESS THE MESSAGE.

Research shows the average prospect needs to hear a message seven times before they take action. Employees don't need quite this same attention—their number is probably closer to three to five times—but it still takes a few reiterations for the message to sink in.

Clearly, repetition is your friend. I often say, "If you're getting tired of delivering your message, then good for you. That means you're doing your job."

Beyond repetition, you should develop messages based on your audience's needs and then communicate with them in multiple ways. Engage key influencers and thought leaders along with supervisors throughout the organization. When employees hear the same messages from their supervisor (always their preferred source for job-related information), from the CEO, read it on the intranet, and hear it through the grapevine, they're more likely to believe it and, most important, act on it.

You should also remember that getting information out is just that—getting information out. Nothing more. To truly communicate, you need to know that the information was received and understood. In fact, doing a little and thinking you are done is one of the most common traps I see leaders fall into. The downside is a lack of information, skepticism, mistrust, confusion, or worse yet, inaction among those you are trying to reach.

? WHAT'S THE BEST PIECE OF ADVICE YOU'VE RECEIVED IN YOUR CAREER

Advice:
Ask for help BEFORE there's a crisis.

Back Story: In my first manager role, I felt that I had to be able to handle everything to earn credibility with my new colleagues. But I couldn't possibly do everything alone, and I ended up having to ask for help on a project after I had waited too long and things were getting out of control. A senior executive took me aside and told me that asking for help was actually a sign of strength, not weakness.

Outcome: I learned that I could ask for help when I needed it—without hurting my credibility. I also learned that surrounding yourself with people who are better than you in one area or another is essential in leadership. Business is a team sport, not an individual one. We all need help. I often work with people who are new to a leadership role, and one of the first things I share with them is that raising your hand and asking for help is the right thing to do.

Anne C. Toulouse
Vice President,
Global Brand Management
and Advertising,
The Boeing Company

SEND MESSAGES THAT ARE MISSING FUNDAMENTAL DETAILS.

All too often, we forget important information when we communicate and only share part of the story. We might miss the context or what it means to our team.

DO ✓

CHECK AND VERIFY THAT YOUR MESSAGE IS COMPLETE.

Any journalist can tell you about the 5 Ws and an H, essential ingredients in any solid news story. You can use these same six questions when communicating with your employees to ensure you're not missing an important detail, that you're sharing the all-important context, and that the communication is relevant for your audience:

What: What's the decision? What does it mean? What should I know? What's in it for me?

Why: Why is it the right decision? Why now? Why is it important?

Where: Where is the decision coming from? Where/what locations will it affect? Where can I get more information?

When: When is this happening?

How: How was the decision made? How will it be implemented? How will communications flow internally and externally? How does it impact me?

Who: Who made the decision? Who's in charge? Who does it impact?

In communicating your message, the order is important. Adult learners want to know the "what" first and then the "why." The rest can follow logically.

Another Great Communication Planning Tool

Just as you have an ongoing plan for continuous improvement in your business, you should have a plan to continuously improve how you communicate with employees. You can ensure continuous improvement in your communication by applying The Deming Cycle, a common continuous improvement process that began with an industrial production focus but has been adopted to drive business strategy. It's often found as an underpinning of Six Sigma or Kaizen improvement programs.

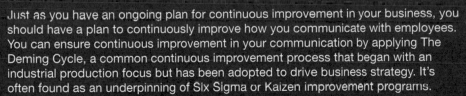

Plan: Establish business and communication objectives to deliver expected results.

Do: Implement new communication processes, often on a small scale if possible.

Check: Measure new communication processes and compare results against the expected results.

Act: Analyze differences to determine their cause. Apply changes for continuous improvement.

? WHAT'S THE BEST PIECE OF ADVICE YOU'VE RECEIVED IN YOUR CAREER

Advice:
Surround yourself with people greater than you and give them the credit. That fosters growth of the best future executives.

Carl Chaney
Retired, President and
Chief Executive Officer,
Hancock Holding Company

-DON'T- ⊘USE ONLY ONE METHOD TO DELIVER A MESSAGE.

Relying on only one form of communication—such as a monthly email message or webcast—is a clear mistake if you want to have maximum impact. Employees have different personalities and work habits.

-DO- ✓CONSIDER HOW YOUR EMPLOYEES LIKE TO RECEIVE INFORMATION.

No matter how much you may like one form of communication, you need to communicate with employees in their chosen medium.

Some people need to hear messaging in person. For others, the written word will sink in best. Some employees always check their email, while others look to social networks for the latest news and communication. Never assume that one message delivered one way will resonate with everyone. You might need to communicate the same message in multiple ways to reach and be heard and understood by everyone. Think of communication as a system and consider all the pieces and parts that make up that system.

CHAPTER FOUR: Be a Two-Way Communicator

Lessons from Preschool Story Time.

During a recent trip to the local bookstore with my 5-year-old daughter, Avi, we sat down for a storytelling session in the children's section. The facilitator, looking like a giant on a pint-sized blue chair, began with a simple question: "What do we need to do to get started, kids?"

The preschoolers and kindergarteners seated in a semi-circle responded in unison. "Open our ears, close our mouths, eyes on me (the facilitator)." I thought to myself, "Holy cow! That can work for leaders, too."

If you want to exude presence and improve how you communicate, it starts with really listening. Leaders with that "wow factor," that "je ne sais quoi" have learned how to be present. They are in the moment and listen more than they talk. Listening carefully helps them gather valuable information, demonstrate that they care, and ultimately draws people to them.

That deep listening sets the stage for great leaders to inspire on a range of other levels, too. They often follow their listening skills with other critical approaches for commanding a room.

- They are self-aware and true to themselves. They know how they can make a difference, and are authentic.

- They have a voice. They speak clearly and can articulate what they mean in easily understandable terms.

- They can read their audience. They tune in to others and present their ideas in ways that resonate with the group. They ask open-ended questions to gather helpful information.

- They tell stories and make connections. Rather than speaking in platitudes, they relate experiences from their own lives that help the audience see them as human, relatable and as people they want to follow.

- They are inspirational and get their message across. They imagine the future and motivate others to join.

- They manage their emotions. They respond rather than react to others.

- They are aware of their body language and the cues of others. They have strong posture, eye contact, use an appropriate tone, and match their words and actions. They exude passion. They have an abundance of energy, are positive and share their enthusiasm with others.

- They understand their own leadership style but can easily read and adapt to the style of others.

- They connect with others as opposed to just transacting with them. They understand that everything they say or do communicates something, and use that fact to be influential with others.

Presence isn't something you're just born with. Sure, it may come more naturally for some people, but it's also easily developed as long as you're willing to work at it. When it comes down to it, it's really about just digging in and really listening—ears open, mouths closed, eyes on them all.

What should you keep doing to increase your presence, and what do you need to start doing?

⊘ DON'T — SKIP RIGHT TO THE PUNCH LINE.

One of the most common mistakes for leaders is jumping into a message without helping employees understand where you're coming from. It's one of the easiest ways for you to shut down or confuse employees.

✓ DO — SET THE CONTEXT.

One of the core responsibilities of a leader in helping their employees with line-of-sight and sound decision-making is to set the proper context (the other is to make information relevant). As you think about how to set context, below are some of the categories of information to consider. Ask yourself…to understand what's happening and why, does your team need information on:

- Background/history
- Strategy and objectives
- Metrics/success
- Relative priority
- Assumptions
- Reasons behind decisions
- Roles
- Knowledge of the stakes

REMEMBER: *Go Slow to go fast.* Providing the right insights and making them relevant to your outcome up front will help your staff make sound decisions and avoid false starts and re-work. When mistakes happen, ask yourself, "What context did I fail to set?"

WITHOUT CONTEXT,
THERE'S NO MEANING

Every employee comes into the workplace with his or her own context. It's a mix of our upbringing, culture, religion, memories, and experiences, along with our other cues and clues from the individual communicating the message. Context influences how we interpret information. It's the glasses through which we look at and understand the world. For example, without context, our business plan is simply words on a page with little if any meaning.

Part of the role we have as leaders is to create a shared vision. That requires a common understanding of context from those who will help us achieve our goals. For example, how do we view the current business situation we're in, and why does the plan just developed make sense? Setting context might involve talking about our current results and management expectations, new customer requirements, and data…all of which help us understand the current situation, or in other words, the "why" behind the plan.

So if you want to get from blank stare to "ah-ha," connect the dots between what you say and what the listener already knows. Set the context in terms of where the listener is coming from so they have the big picture to understand and contribute in a meaningful way.

WHAT'S THE **BEST** PIECE OF ADVICE YOU'VE RECEIVED IN YOUR CAREER

Advice:
Share mutual respect.

Back Story: I think it's so important to develop a mutual respect and openness among leaders and communicators. Communicators need to be 100 percent honest with their leaders about the questions and feedback they're getting from employees—no matter how difficult it may be to share it. In turn, leaders need to listen carefully to that feedback (not just hear it), and be 100 percent honest with their communicators about their own perspective and motivations, and what they feel can be shared with the entire organization, and when.

Outcome: When the two truly understand each other and know the approach they plan to take to a sensitive or difficult situation, it's that much easier for both of them to communicate in the most effective ways. When that doesn't happen, I've seen that the messages can either bleed out or bleed in. Either way, that's damaging to the organization.

Jim Amorosia
CEO, Motel 6

SHUT IDEAS DOWN.

Leaders often fall into the trap of thinking they have all the answers: "I'm the one with the vision and I know what my people need. I don't need to hear their opinions."

Yet the fastest way to lose employees' confidence and trust is to make them feel their opinions don't matter. We all need to resist our egos.

DO ✓

BE OPEN TO NEW IDEAS AND SEEK THEM OUT.

Good leaders know that soliciting and listening to the opinions of employees can be a great way to gain honest insights and valuable new perspectives.

Always remember, communication is a two-way street. As leaders, it's essential to nurture open lines of communication and dialogue, and actually listen to people's ideas at every level of the organization.

A few key pointers:

- Stop talking
- Simply state: "I want to hear different perspectives on this"
- Purposefully solicit views from the quietest people in the room
- Listen with an open mind, not for what you want to hear
- Use multiple vehicles to solicit opinions—face-to-face meetings, focus groups, manager forums, emails, employee surveys
- Listen for what people say and also watch for body language and non-verbal cues

Courage is what it takes to stand up and speak: courage is also what it takes to sit down and listen."

- Winston Churchill.

DON'T ⊘ JUST PASS ALONG A MEMO.

Sending along a note from your boss to your team with no context surely won't resonate with employees, especially on the important matters that mean so much to driving the business forward.

DO ✓ MAKE IT RELEVANT FOR YOUR TEAM.

Don't be a copy-cat communicator. Your job is to take information and make it relevant for your employees.

Help them understand what it means for the team. Customize and personalize the message so your team knows why it matters to them and what they need to do. Only you can do that for your team. No one else can.

Relevant means:
- Pertinent
- Meaningful
- Connected
- Related to me and my job

DON'T
⊘ ASSUME YOU UNDERSTAND.

In the fast-paced environments in which we all work, it's easy to make quick assumptions about points our colleagues make. It's also common for colleagues to talk at one another.

DO ✓
PLAY BACK WHAT YOU'RE HEARING.

As leaders, we need to regularly paraphrase what we hear. That helps us know we're understanding what's been said, and lets others know they've been heard.

You can check your understanding with phrases such as, "If I'm understanding you, you're saying..." or "Tell me if this is what you're saying..."

ASK CLOSED-ENDED QUESTIONS.

It's so important to ask the right kind of engaging questions if you want be a two-way communicator. Recently, I was coaching a leader on strategic presentation skills. He had the tendency to keep talking without stopping and needed some work to better connect with the people in the room.

We talked about the importance of pausing during the presentation and asking a question to engage the audience. During our coaching session, when he first paused for emphasis, I was happy he had listened to my recommendation. But then he counteracted the positive effect by asking, "Does anyone have any questions?" That's like saying, "Does anyone want to loan me $5,000?" It was great for him to pause, but asking a closed-ended question basically shut people down rather than opening them up.

DO ✓

ASK OPEN-ENDED QUESTIONS.

One sure way to fuel conversations is with open-ended questions. Unlike questions that give people limited options for response, open-ended questions encourage others to express their opinions and ideas. When you listen to what they have to say, showing interest and respect for their input, it shows you care. The impact can be significant.

Try these open-ended questions in your next presentation or conversation:

- Who can share reactions to what I just said?
- What's your feedback on the choices I just presented?
- What are your thoughts?
- Would you tell me more about_____?
- Can you help me understand that a little better?
- How does that process work now?
- How do you see this happening?
- What kind of challenges are you facing?
- What's the most important priority to you with this? Why?
- What other issues are important to you?
- What is it that you'd like to see accomplished?

WHAT'S THE BEST PIECE OF ADVICE YOU'VE RECEIVED IN YOUR CAREER

Advice:
Ask good questions. They can change the world.

Back Story: As a young student at Georgetown University, I was struck by how many times our Jesuit professors would invoke the same eight words: "The questions are more important than the answers."

At first, my response was, "Yeah, and you're the ones asking the endless questions." But as I explored their words more carefully, it became clear to me what the Jesuits meant. They were prompting us to think, to query accepted norms, and push beyond the mundane to get to a better answer that would provide us with a deeper understanding. Think about it. If no one questioned norms or accepted conventional wisdom, we might still believe that the earth is flat and that the universe revolves around us. That might mean that we never know enough to travel to other lands or help others through science and other means. No medicine, no telecommunications, no computers and no internet. No means even to easily communicate with you about this idea from afar.

As I've aged and had the opportunity to lead teams as the chief communications officer at five large U.S.-based companies, I've learned the power of inquiry in yet a second way. Bad questions can demotivate a person or a team and good questions can help them achieve greatness.

Outcome: Many executives – in the name of keeping their teams on task and driving for accountability – ask probing questions. Yet too often, those questions can be disempowering. Take these for instance:

- "Why are you behind schedule?"
- "Can't you make this work?"
- "What's taking the team so long?"
- "Why don't you do it this way?"
- "Are you sure we have the right people on this?"

Such questions tend to shut people down, make them defensive and get them focused on not making mistakes, as opposed to playing to win. Telling people what to do is never as effective as asking good questions that help your employees discover what is best to do.

Whether it is getting a team focused on a major project, creating a new online tool, or navigating a crisis, I've found that guiding with questions is much more effective. In that kind of environment, employees are empowered, share ownership and responsibility for getting things done well, are more creative and innovative, and take greater pride in their work. By asking the right questions, we can help them remove mental blocks and refocus them on the possibilities and opportunities. Better questions, depending on the circumstances, might be:

- "What are the benefits we are striving for here on behalf of (pick a valued stakeholder customor or otherwise)?"
- "What are you most pleased with thus far?"
- "What additional help or resources might be helpful to bring this project to closure?"
- "Are there other uses for what you and your team are creating here?"
- "What key things need to happen for you to meet with your objectives?"
- "How can I help?"

This kind of open questioning has helped Cargill leaders transform our relationships with employees and our clients. We're all learning from the wisdom and the power of the Jesuits: the questions are indeed better than the answers.

Mike Fernandez
Corporate Vice President,
Cargill

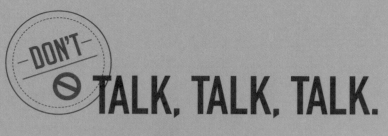

DON'T

🚫 TALK, TALK, TALK.

Employees are bombarded
with information but starved for
meaning. Don't just talk at them,
as they'll be sure to tune out.

LISTEN AND CREATE DIALOGUE.

Listening is a skill virtually all of us can work on. There are a number of ways to raise the bar when it comes to truly listening.

Follow these steps to become a better listener:

- Approach each dialogue with the goal to learn something. Think, "This person can teach me something."

- Stop talking and focus closely on the speaker. Suppress the urge to multitask or think about what you are going to say next

- Open and guide the conversation with broad, open-ended questions, such as, "How do you envision…" or "Help me understand how you're thinking about this."

- Then, drill down to the details, where needed, by asking direct, specific questions that focus the conversation, such as "Tell me more about…," "How would this work?" or "What challenges might we face?"

- Pay attention to your responses. Be aware of your body language and recognize that the way you respond to a question will facilitate further dialogue or limit what's discussed by shutting someone down. Purposefully let someone know you're listening and want to hear more from them through positive body or other verbal cues.

- Summarize what you're hearing and ask questions to confirm your understanding, such as "Here's what I hear you saying…" or "Let me summarize what I'm hearing…"

- Listen for total meaning. Recognize that, in addition to what is being said, the real message may be non-verbal; consider what's not being said as critical to the message, too.

In the end, the goal is to better understand where someone is coming from and get the information you need to take the next step and/or make a smart decision.

One of the greatest skills that any leader can master is becoming comfortable with silence. Many people view silence as empty space that needs to be filled, but when leaders learn to accept it—and work with it—they open the door for others to speak and be heard. The result is often unexpected and enlightening, and a wealth of information.

? | WHAT'S THE BEST PIECE OF ADVICE YOU'VE RECEIVED IN YOUR CAREER

Advice:
Humans were created with twice as many listening devices (ears!) as noisemakers (our big mouths), and the capability to use only one or the other at a time with any success. When in doubt, majority rules: listen before and more than you talk.

Advice:
Work your tail off, and have fun doing it. There's no crime in enjoying the people you work with, laughing with them and creating an environment where people want to give it their all. Your work will be better, more fulfilling and more impactful.

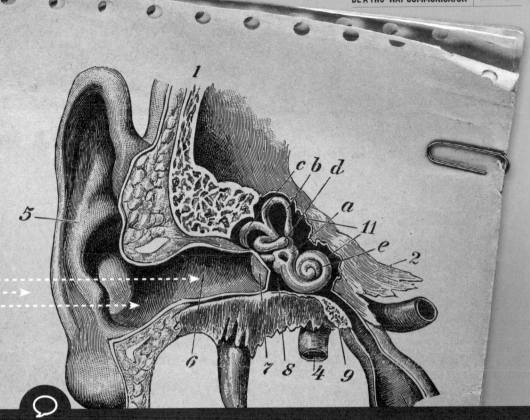

Advice:
If you're going to fall, fail forward. Taking calculated risks with eyes wide open is often where real innovation happens. But you have to be willing to try, willing to fail, and willing to learn from the experience. The reason is simple: the world is moving too quickly to maintain the status quo, which is the fastest way to fall behind.

Howard N. Karesh, APR
Vice President,
Corporate Communications,
Hill-Rom Holdings, Inc.

CHAPTER FIVE:
Cut
Through
The Clutter

Building A True Culture Of Communication.

A report released this year from the market research firm Gallup[10] reinforced something I've long believed: leaders who embrace communication build truly engaged and inspired workforces.

Gallup found that workers whose managers are consistent communicators—holding regular, informative meetings—are three times more likely to feel committed and enthusiastic about their jobs.

Workers also told Gallup that they wanted to be in contact with supervisors daily, and not just about the daily business happenings. They also liked to see bosses take an interest in their personal lives. Employees who feel they can communicate openly tend to place deep trust in their bosses, said Jim Harter, chief scientist for Gallup's workplace and wellbeing research, in a *Wall Street Journal* piece about the study.

As that survey and many others have shown us over the years, there's tremendous power in communicating at a deep level with employees. At the same time, we all know that the employee engagement journey is a continuous one. Communication is not an "event." It is a continuing process. You must work every day to ask the right questions, answer others appropriately, and communicate openly and honestly with employees. When they see you are making that extra effort, they'll do the same. By moving away from lip service and toward positive action, you drive positive business results.

Organizations that understand, prioritize, and constantly strive to achieve better internal communication are a breed apart. They achieve trust and credibility. They enable employees to do their jobs better. They create a constructive workplace that encourages growth and a common sense of purpose.

From all this, there can only be one result: higher levels of performance and better business results.

What one thing can you do to further engage with your team?

DON'T HIDE IN YOUR OFFICE.

DO ROUNDS.

It's a basic theory—and it works. Allocate time each month to walk the halls, eat lunch in the cafeteria, talk face-to-face with the factory manager or employees on the floor.

Ensure that on every trip, you spend time talking with employees at the location. Schedule these activities in your calendar, just like any other appointment.

A company president who I work with makes a point when visiting sites to talk with everyone who's working there. While he meets with management too, he dedicates much of his time to frontline employees. He learns from them, and everyone knows one of his top priorities is the people who interact every day with that organization's customers. Successful leaders make rounds because they understand this truth: It's easier for people to trust you when they get to know and see you. Let people see you, be present in multiple ways, and get to know others—and let them get to know you, too.

Keep in mind that your interactions with employees also need to include remote workers. Use technology appropriately to create channels of communication so that employees can reach out to you when they have a question, concern or idea. Don't commit to this, however, unless you plan to answer the questions or emails yourself. Employees know canned responses or those that don't sound like they're coming from you.

MANAGEMENT BY WALKING AROUND
(A.K.A. LEADERSHIP)

If you want to know what's going on with your team, ask. Typically, the biggest barrier to walking around is the fear of doing it, and specifically, knowing what to ask. Not to mention the myth of time: "I don't have time to do it." The reality is that if you thought it was important, you'd make the time (and then make the most of that time).

Here are the open-ended questions that are sure-fire ways to get close to your team members and understand how things are going:

- What's keeping you up at night?

- What are you working on?

- What's most exciting to you right now?

- Give me one thing that's going well… and something that could be better

- What's one skill you're working on today from a development standpoint?

- I always appreciate tough questions. What's a tough question you have for me?

CONNECTING WITH
REMOTE WORKERS

In this world where so many of us are connected 24/7 through technology, there are still many employees who—believe it or not—are hard to reach. I'm talking about people who have limited face-to-face visibility with senior leaders or even with their supervisors. Hard-to-reach employees may be working in remote offices, constantly on the move away from their home base, or on a production floor without phone or email access. They may be part of a global organization that has team members literally in different worlds—across various continents, cultures, and time zones.

Like any communication challenge, connecting with hard-to-reach employees starts with knowing your audience, then understanding how they want to get information.

- What is important to them and how is it best communicated?

- What attracts their attention and what doesn't?

- How can you help connect the dots between their work and the company's goals?

With numbers of hard-to-reach and remote workers growing and communication a critical part of a supervisor's job, leaders need to ask some critical questions to be sure resources are applied where they should be.

As much as they may appreciate the convenience it offers, people who work remotely can feel far removed from their colleagues in the office. They still need the human connection, conversation and insight of the workplace even when they are miles away or on the shop floor. Here are tips for helping remote workers feel included and valued:

- **Communicate predictably.** Be more strategic about when you'll communicate. Out of sight can mean out of mind, so ensure that's not the case. Set regular meeting times and agree on how the team will interact outside the meetings. This lets remote workers know when to expect feedback and how best to follow up with colleagues and leaders.

- **Respond quickly.** An afternoon can seem like an eternity to a remote worker who is waiting for your input or response but can't see that you are busy or in an all-day meeting. Even a quick email acknowledgment saying when you can respond is helpful. Consider sharing your daily calendar with employees so they see when you're in meetings or out of the office.

- **Appreciate frequently.** The little things mean a lot to an employee who has few interactions with their manager or colleagues. Show appreciation for good work and notice when remote employees deliver what you need or respond quickly. Highlight the successes of remote workers via company communications and the intranet.

- **Pick up the phone more often to touch base.** Hearing your voice and knowing that you took the time to reach out shows remote workers that they are still valued.

- **Email important company news updates** to remote workers, including links to intranet sites that feature and compile the highlights in one place.

- **Plan regular shift meetings** so supervisors can share company updates with employees.

- **Use group text messaging to your advantage** to deliver critical or urgent news to highly mobile workers.

- **Train supervisors to improve their communication skills with remote workers.** Wherever they are, employees need to hear important messages repeatedly for them to sink in.

- **Keep in mind that employees want leaders who listen to their needs.** Employees need to know that their voices are heard, whether they work remotely or not.

-DON'T-
⊘ ASSUME YOUR EMPLOYEES UNDERSTAND YOUR STRATEGY.

You might have the most compelling vision for your organization, but if you can't get it out of your head and get others to see it and believe in it, it might as well not even exist.

_DO_ ✓

CODIFY THE STRATEGY AND COMMUNICATE ABOUT IT REGULARLY.

Just because the strategy makes sense to you doesn't mean it will take only an instant for others to see it like you do.

We often think that others think as we do, that others see the world as we do, but it's more likely that there's a lot of ground to cover between their perspective and yours. Employees come to their jobs with their own context, and it's the leader's job to help them understand the collective context, including how you see the marketplace today, and how that led to your strategy.

According to our research, a majority of employees globally don't understand their company's strategy and, as a consequence, how they fit in. Consider the possibilities from having even 10 or 20 percent more employees understanding their jobs better. What might the impact be on productivity, innovation, or revenue?

It's up to you to engage others so they have the same clear picture you do of your strategy and where the business is going. The reality is that some may have small windows into your view of the strategy, but very few have the whole picture like you do. Lift the perspective out of your head and get it into others' so they can own it and help you achieve it.

WHAT'S THE **BEST** PIECE OF ADVICE YOU'VE RECEIVED IN YOUR CAREER

Advice:
Define what work-life balance means to you by setting clear and reasonable expectations (and live them).

Back Story: When you work in a non-profit, it's easy to lose your perspective on work-life balance because you're so driven and motivated by the cause you're promoting through your organization. Leaders in non-profits, in particular, run the risk of overworking themselves, mistakenly believing that anything short of a 60- to 80-hour work week demonstrates a lack of dedication to the mission at hand. Then, add a Type A personality, such as myself, to the mix; now you really have a work overload situation!

This was my case, and all along, it's as if I had secretly wished some caring leader would take notice and intervene, helping me limit the extremes I was facing—all while not perceiving me as weak. It never happened.

Outcome: I helped myself. I finally decided to take personal responsibility for my own wellbeing. You might say it was my "aha" moment. I realized the best person to create a healthy lifestyle and boundaries for me, *was me*; and that by doing so, everyone benefited such as my family, friends and yes—even co-workers. I came to my conclusion when it dawned on me that my people want me to be at my best for them and in order to do that, I had to be the best for me. My staff and direct reports deserve my undivided attention; they deserve a good role model and they deserve good leadership.

But let's face it—no leader is made out of steel and I'm no exception. I had to redefine my priorities; I had to set clear and high, but reasonable expectations. Most importantly, I had to articulate and live out this new conviction, ensuring that my words matched my actions. You can't give what you don't have. Today, I can say with confidence that is not my case and my personal and professional life are better for it.

Mark Yeadon
Senior Vice President
of Global Program,
Compassion International

WAYS TO BRING YOUR
STRATEGY TO LIFE.

- **Put the strategy on a single piece of paper.** Let it serve as a strategic framework from which all leaders and employees operate.

- **Share the strategic framework and ensure your leaders are aligned.** Give leaders the context behind the strategy so they understand how you got there. Ask them to make the strategy relevant for their teams.

- **Use the strategic framework consistently in your communications with employees.** That way, it becomes familiar to employees and they see what's happening and how it ties to the strategy. They'll know what's important when they see and hear it from multiple sources.

- **As your thinking evolves about the strategy (quarterly, annually, etc.), update your framework and communicate regularly** so employees are in the loop and understand the reasons behind decisions.

- **Celebrate "wins,"** always connecting back to and reinforcing the core elements of the strategy.

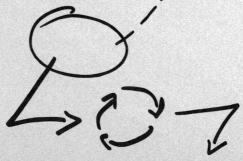

THINK OF YOUR STRATEGY
AS A JOURNEY.

Before you embark on a journey, there are many considerations and details to plan. The more you prepare and plan, the more enjoyable and fruitful your journey will be (and you'll get to your destination faster).

- **Help employees understand why the journey is a good idea for the organization and for them as individuals.** Explain the "why" behind a plan or change, including current results, new customer requirements, and recently acquired competitive data that boosts the credibility of the "why."

- **Define the destination.** Get employees excited and help them envision the destination. Articulate the goal with clear performance benchmarks and data.

- **Explain the "how"**—or what you expect of employees. Help them to understand their role in reaching the destination. Detail the behaviors you seek, and explain how those behaviors will deliver the desired results. Provide a road map and explain where there may be challenges throughout the journey, but remind them of the benefits of the destination.

- **Answer the "what's in it for me" question that all employees ask.** They need to know that the destination will be as beneficial for them as it will be for the company or others within the company.

- **Log the journey.** Seek feedback along the way. Listen for the right messages to be played back to you so that you feel confident your employees are on the right path to the destination. Allow them to ask questions and seek clarity on why one road is better than another.

- **By predicting and answering the who, what, when, where, why and how questions,** you will enable your workforce to understand the context and relevancy of your strategy. Preparation and regular communications will help you have a smooth journey and arrive at your destination on time and ready to enjoy the adventure.

GIVE SIGNALS THAT YOU DON'T CARE.

It's a truism—how you say something often trumps what you say.

Language psychologist Albert Mehrabian's famous research[11] breaks communication into three distinct categories: words, tone of voice, and body language. He concludes that when a speaker's body language and tone of voice are at odds with the words used, the audience tends to give much more credence to the body language and tone of voice.

In those cases where there's such incongruence, Mehrabian concluded that the audience pays far more attention to the nonverbal portions of the message. Those nonverbal portions account for 93 percent of the total meaning. Conversely, the words said in those situations carry little meaning—just 7 percent of the total meaning. Clearly, our non-verbal communication carries a lot of power— inspiring confidence or sending signals of uncertainty and doubt.

— DO —
✓

PAY ATTENTION TO YOUR BODY LANGUAGE.

Leaders need to be aware of what they may be communicating nonverbally, whether it is intentional or not.

Here are tried-and-true strategies to send the signal you intend:

- **Watch others**—Start as a keen observer of others. Watch presenters or leaders you admire and see how they engage others through verbal and nonverbal communication. Note what works and what doesn't.

- **Evaluate yourself**—Use a mirror to watch your facial expressions. Even better, record yourself interacting with others, informally or formally, and decide what changes you may need to make. Watching yourself on videotape is a powerful way to observe yourself in action and note any blind spots you have, or identify signals you're sending that you don't intend.

- **Check with others**—Ask someone you trust if they notice any nonverbal cues that may give the wrong impression.

- **Practice**—Answer questions and make statements in front of the mirror or camera until you are comfortable delivering a sincere message with continuous eye contact.

MODEL THE BEST BODY LANGUAGE BEHAVIORS REGULARLY.

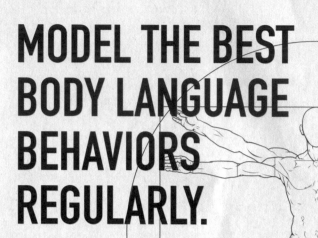

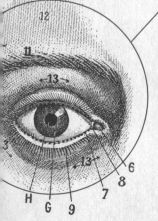

MAKE STRONG EYE CONTACT

Regular eye contact builds relationships and inspires confidence. Looking someone in the eye during a conversation shows respect and interest in what they have to say. If you look away, it can be interpreted as a lack of confidence or give the impression you are lying. It's also important that leaders turn away from their laptops, tablets and smartphones when they are speaking directly to employees. This demonstrates focus and shows your teams that you genuinely care about what they have to say.

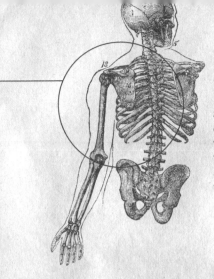

PRACTICE GOOD POSTURE

Stand and sit up straight to show you are relaxed and in command of a situation. Whatever your actual height may be, you will make a positive impression if you stand, walk and sit tall. Holding your head high indicates open-mindedness and attentiveness. Even if people see you from a distance they will get the message that you are confident and in control.

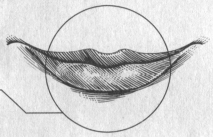

USE POSITIVE EXPRESSIONS

Your facial expressions and body positions are like pictures that paint a thousand words. A smile engages people and promotes positive interaction. Being still, leaning forward and focusing on the person in front of you demonstrates interest and suggests you are open to what they have to say. The opposite impression is given by crossing your arms or legs, hunching shoulders forward and having a rigid posture. If you are trying to connect with people who present this "closed" position, ask them about themselves or their concerns and listen to what they have to say.

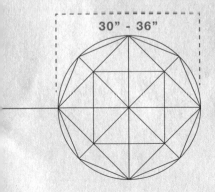

RESPECT PERSONAL SPACE AND POSITION

People can become uncomfortable if you encroach on their personal space, which typically ranges between 30 and 36 inches. Consider this when setting chairs for meetings as well as in one-on-one interactions. Also remember seating positions can send a message. Placing chairs at a 45-degree angle to one another tends to encourage collaboration, while having a desk or table between people can be a barrier to teamwork.

WHAT'S THE BEST PIECE OF ADVICE YOU'VE RECEIVED IN YOUR CAREER

Advice:
Smile more.

Back Story: I was the first finance executive hired by a company that had historically promoted from within. The culture was much softer than cultures I had experienced; creativity, accountability and new ideas had stalled, which hindered growth and productivity. So, they decided to hire leadership from different backgrounds to increase urgency and accountability. I was from competitive, results-focused companies with tough cultures, and I took the job purposefully to soften those edges. It was hard to adapt at first. My mentor, a senior woman with the company for some time, had these two words of advice—smile more.

Outcome: I was offended. I was a serious business woman, but since it came from a woman I respected, I tried. It felt so unnatural at first. I am very focused at work, and I LOOK focused, which is often incorrectly interpreted as unhappiness. I felt downright silly at business meetings smiling for no real reason, but changes started. People smiled back at me and began to relax with me. Smiling at work quickly became more natural, and I actually began to feel happier and less stressed despite still being focused. Now I smile a lot, and the results keep coming!

Terri Luckett
Chief Financial Officer,
Terminal Investments,
Limited S.A

JUST SEEK FEEDBACK.

If you're insincere about collecting feedback, you'll erode trust and you won't be able to move your business forward.

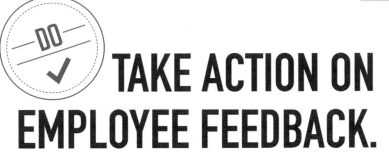

TAKE ACTION ON EMPLOYEE FEEDBACK.

Once you ask your team for feedback, and they've responded with honest, considerate input, you might be thinking…now what? As a leader, when your employees share their thoughts, the work is just beginning. This is the time when you need to take action on their feedback.

No matter whether you plan to implement their suggestions or not, you need to close the loop with employees to let them know one of the following:

1. You're implementing their solution, and the rationale

2. You're implementing a modified version of their suggestion, and the rationale for that

3. You're not planning to implement their solution, and the rationale for that

In all cases, cover what you plan to do and why. This helps employees know how you think (what guides your decision-making), which allows them to think more like you in the future. It also might open a conversation for how others might ask you to think differently about a specific problem or opportunity. Sometimes, leaders complain of survey fatigue, worrying that employees will tune out if asked to fill out another survey. However, if you show a genuine commitment to act on feedback, you won't have trouble getting employees to provide it.

Finally, when you communicate about the solution, don't forget to mention where the idea came from and recognize the employee for their valuable perspective. When employees know their input is heard and valued, they will be more willing to share their feedback in the future. They will also feel more engaged when they know their thoughts and insights are valued. Soliciting employee feedback is one thing, but the proof that you take it seriously comes from taking action.

DON'T

TRY TO BE SOMEONE YOU'RE NOT THROUGH SOCIAL MEDIA.

You don't want to force yourself to use a particular social media tool just because you think it projects a certain image of you as hip or progressive.

If you're a thoughtful leader who likes to speak in more detail, Twitter is not your go-to platform. Instead, a compelling blog with a conversational tone might be the better option.

DO

FIND YOUR AUTHENTIC SOCIAL MEDIA VOICE.

Your conversations in social media need to reflect you and your personality.

Just as employees can sense when a leader is disengaged or avoiding a difficult topic, they can sniff out enterprise social media conversations that appear inauthentic or robotic. For instance, if someone on the communications team is writing your blog for you, ensure that your voice is reflected well and that you come across as sincere and true to your personality and passions.

-DON'T- 🚫TRY TO STIFLE DIALOGUE ON SOCIAL MEDIA.

If employees don't trust that you're looking for honest feedback on platforms or that you're open to tough questions, the tool will become far less effective in driving change and improvements within your company.

Employees will opt-out of conversations because they fear reprisals and reprimands for asking authentic—but sometimes tough—questions of their leaders.

-DO- ✓WORK TOWARD OPEN, HONEST DIALOGUE ON SOCIAL MEDIA.

Nothing is more important than building trust in your conversations.

A high degree of trust can yield the healthy, robust dialogue that helps employees feel an even stronger connection to their employer. The more they're trusted to speak directly and honestly with their leaders via socially-enhanced platforms, the more they feel a sense of ownership and inclusion in the company's strategic journey.

🚫 DIVE INTO ANY AND ALL SOCIAL MEDIA PLATFORMS JUST TO "KEEP UP."

No matter where I travel, leaders and communicators wonder the same thing: When it comes to social media, am I doing enough to keep up?

That leads some leaders to jump in too quickly with tools that don't fit their personal style or the company's culture. Never rush in without some careful consideration for what will work best for you and your employees.

CUT THROUGH THE CLUTTER

BE THOUGHTFUL ABOUT YOUR USE OF SOCIAL MEDIA.

If you're looking to add social media platforms to communicate with employees, there are plenty of options.

However, social media is not a one-size-fits-all proposition, so you'll need to pick the right tool for each conversation. You wouldn't announce a wide-scale company restructuring in an email. The company Intranet sharing site is not the place for that kind of announcement either. With difficult or controversial discussions, there's no replacement for the face-to-face conversation.

You'll also want to pick social media forums that reflect your philosophy, comfort level and sense of professionalism. For instance, friending an employee on Facebook might be appropriate if you've already got a strong presence there and you regularly post updates on your company. It may also make sense to friend employees if you're already encouraging your teams to be social ambassadors for the company. However, friend requests might not be appropriate for many other leaders looking to separate their personal lives from their professional ones. In those cases, a LinkedIn connection might be a better fit.

In making these choices as a leader, keep in mind that some tools provide more social involvement than others. For instance, a leader blog tends to be static—and less social— if it simply amplifies your perspective in a one-way broadcast. But the moment that you encourage dialogue through commenting and sharing, the communication becomes much more social and is clearly enhanced by social media.

Enterprise Social Media Could Include:

- Company blogs
- Intranet articles that enable commenting, sharing or liking
- Team sites for collaboration and idea exchange
- Social platforms like Yammer, Chatter or Jive
- Company-curated (member only) LinkedIn networks
- Behind-the-firewall video channels
- Other opt-in conversation and collaboration sites (now commonly built into intranet platforms like SharePoint)

? | WHAT'S THE
BEST
PIECE OF ADVICE
YOU'VE RECEIVED
IN YOUR CAREER

Advice:
If you always have to be right, there is no space for anyone else in the room.

Back Story: The best leadership advice I ever received came from an early mentor in my career, Ron Saba. He was a terrific guy with keen social acumen. His advice was this: *"If you always have to be right, there is no space for anyone else in the room."*

Outcome: What he really meant was you may be right but if you can't communicate it well and bring others along you may as well call it quits.

Maribeth Malloy
Director Environmental Sustainability & External Engagement,
Lockheed Martin

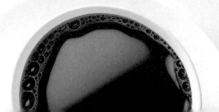

DON'T ASSUME PEOPLE KNOW YOUR EXPECTATIONS.

My mom often used to say to me, "I'm not a mind reader. You have to talk to me. You may think I know what you're thinking, but I don't." The same is true for your employees—they can't read your minds, which means you have to communicate with them!

SHARE YOUR EXPECTATIONS, NEEDS AND HOPES.

When expectations are shared, research shows that employees most often rise to the occasion. It's a common trap to think that you have shared your expectations. Put them in writing and come back to them often with your team.

Here are must-do steps to help your employees understand your expectations:

- Tell employees what they can expect from you and what you consistently strive to deliver. Be as specific as possible and discuss what each expectation looks like.

- Share what you expect from employees and ask them to consistently deliver as well.

- For every project, make a commitment to discuss the critical success factors up front: the outcome, roles and responsibilities, timing, milestone check points, approval process, and so on.

- Have an expectations check in when you discuss the status of projects. How is the team doing for each expectation?

- Every day, commit to give at least one employee feedback to reinforce positive behaviors (how he or she is meeting expectations) and/or to extinguish any negative behaviors and suggest alternatives.

- Let your staff know that when they have questions, they need to ask. If they don't have certain information that they need to do their jobs effectively, they must seek it out. Everyone needs to always remember that communication is a two-way street. Both you and your employees must play an active role.

DON'T RELY TOO HEAVILY ON TECHNOLOGY TO COMMUNICATE.

We all know how technology enables communication—email, voicemail, text message, instant message, Twitter…the list goes on. There are more than enough ways to communicate, but too often they add up to message overload for employees.

—DO—
✓ COMMUNICATE
FACE-TO-FACE MORE.

When something is important, nothing compares to communicating face-to-face. When a leader needs to inspire people—or move them to action—the best way to do it is to look people in the eye and help them with exactly what they need to know. Communicating face-to-face sends a message before you say a word. People will not only hear what you are saying, they will perceive the greater meaning of your tone, voice inflection, emotion and body language.

Here are six good reasons for leaders to make the time to communicate face-to-face:

1. Demonstrate importance. Being there in person tells your audience they are important to you and the issue you are discussing is worth your time and theirs. Your focus will get people's attention and increase the potential for your message to be heard.

2. Interpret thoughts and feelings. When you are face-to-face, you can see and respond to people's reactions—like facial expressions and body language—as well as their tone of voice. Leaders have the chance to show they care by asking probing questions and actively listening to understand the audience's perspective. This is especially critical when you need employees to adopt new behaviors to advance your goals, such as in times of change.

3. Enhance credibility and trust. Leaders need to build employee trust to be effective. Face-to-face situations allow you to share your strategy, explain it clearly, and answer questions honestly.

4. Build relationships. Interacting directly with other leaders, managers and employees expands your network and establishes shared experience that can enhance future communication. It also helps create camaraderie that is the basis of cooperation and success across the organization.

5. Gather feedback. Meeting in person helps employees feel valued and gives them a chance to contribute input to organizational strategies and communication. It gives the leader a chance to confirm people's understanding of key issues, identify gaps and encourage ongoing feedback and engagement.

6. Address sensitive issues. You demonstrate respect for employees and a commitment to a successful outcome when you deal with a sensitive issue face-to-face. Whether you are providing specific feedback to increase their success or delivering a tough message, focus on your desired outcome and prepare by understanding the employee's mindset and possible reactions.

CHAPTER SIX: Winning Presentations

Let's Have A Conversation.

One of the things I enjoy most about speaking engagements is the chance to connect with different groups of people and hear what's on their minds. Beyond the work we do with our clients, these presentations and the corresponding dialogue help me stay close to the challenges and opportunities in business today. I'm always learning, and excited to hear about new and different strategies to help leaders and their organizations improve communication, engagement, and business results.

Whatever the venue or purpose, I enjoy involving the audience in a conversation on the given topic—leading a dialogue rather than delivering a speech. I find that engaging people in sharing their experiences and insights:

• Creates a positive energy in the room

• Engenders a sense of community and a feeling that in most cases, we all have similar challenges (we're not alone)

• Provides fantastic learning and teaching moments that extend well beyond the meeting

• Is more enjoyable for everyone involved

Here are five winning strategies to turn your next presentation into a great dialogue:

Your mindset matters. Think: your goal is to create and facilitate dialogue, not to make a presentation.

Understand the audience. Who will be in the room and what is their level of knowledge on your topic? Consider the demographic mix, the level of experience and the audience's mindset. Put yourself in their place and consider how to present your material in a way that will resonate with them and where they're coming from. Adjust your content accordingly.

Energize with participation. In a larger audience, engage the group by asking for a show of hands at various points and invite people to share their examples to illustrate key concepts being presented. Consider involving audience members in an appropriate game or demonstration to highlight a key point in an energizing way. And don't forget those who may be participating by phone or web conference!

Ask for input. Plan to ask open-ended questions at critical junctures to check for understanding and gather information. For internal meetings with colleagues or leaders who may have insight into a challenge you face, ask for perspective on crucial issues or to test key messages.

Simplify and summarize. In a world where everyone is juggling volumes of information every day, less is definitely more when it comes to presenting concepts and ideas. Chances are, your slides have way too much content—most of which is not necessary. Consider using simple, memorable ways to package key concepts (try a visual to make your point) and then amplify your point with real-life examples.

Handouts facilitate learning. We typically provide handouts of my PowerPoint slides to allow participants to take notes, which helps many leaders process and retain information. It also provides a way to share the information covered with others who weren't able to participate.

How can you turn your next presentation into an interactive dialogue?

DON'T BE A STRANGER.

If you fail to get to know anyone in the room before you present, you'll have a much harder time connecting with the audience and what they need from you.

DO CREATE CONNECTIONS.

Before you even arrive at the presentation, it's important to do your homework. Have calls with leaders so you can identify their expectations and truly customize your talk.

For presentations away from your regular location, arrive early enough to have a few pre-meetings with leaders and attendees, learn a few things about the local area, and share some of this information as you introduce yourself and your topic to the audience. Highlighting conversations and relationships with people in the room will show your familiarity, put others at ease and gain you instant credibility.

PHONE IT IN.

A normal amount of energy won't capture the audience. Don't forget the importance of winning over your audience in the first moments that you speak.

DIAL UP YOUR ENERGY BY 10 TO 15 PERCENT.

Presenters with more energy and a genuine sense of confidence naturally draw audiences to them.

Presenters should look at their talk as a chance to capture an audience. It's much like an actor going in for an audition—you have to bring a heightened level of enthusiasm to the task. Turn up the volume on your energy level.

JUST TELL A JOKE AT THE START.

I often hear leaders say they need to tell a joke to get the audience's attention. I'm not sure who suggested this notion, but it's not a helpful strategy for the majority of us. It's risky. The problem is that the leader feels pressure to be funny and the joke often gets delivered in an awkward way.

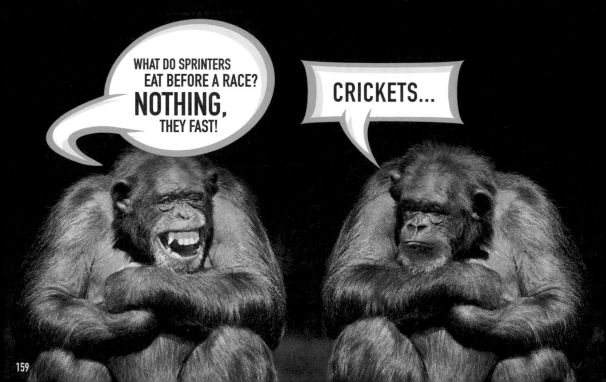

MAKE YOUR START MEMORABLE.

It's critical to get off to a strong start—for you and for the audience. Forget the humor unless you're naturally funny. Even then, skip the joke unless you're 150 percent confident you can deliver flawlessly.

Remember, connecting with the audience by letting them know you understand them and their needs is a winning approach. In my experience, when it comes to presentation style, the audience will cut you slack when your delivery isn't perfect if you have content that they care about.

To start strong, I often recommend memorizing the beginning of your presentation so you can build your confidence right away, like a star forward starting the game with six points on the board. I also compare it to getting on the highway—you have to accelerate to get to the speed you want to arrive at.

Key Pointers For Getting Off To A Great Start:
- **Meet the audience where they are. Help the audience understand why they should listen**
    - Build rapport by telling something about you and why you're passionate about the subject
- **Grab the attention of your audience through a variety of ways:**
    - A short, relevant story
    - A startling statistic or important fact related to the subject
    - Ask a rhetorical question to make the audience think
    - Invite participation and welcome questions
    - In smaller groups, ask what the audience is expecting from the time with you
- **Clearly introduce the topic ahead and why the audience should continue listening intently**

? WHAT'S THE BEST PIECE OF ADVICE YOU'VE RECEIVED IN YOUR CAREER

Advice:
Don't let fear dictate your decisions.

Back Story: Years ago, I was asked to take on a role I shied away from. It was a very large role for me at the time with a lot of responsibility. When I look back on it now, I was afraid of failure.

Outcome: A sage leader told me I had failure mixed up with fear. He explained that taking a risk and it not working was not failure. The real failure was allowing fear to dictate my decisions.

Carolyn M. Rose
Vice President,
Talent Effectiveness,
Rockwell Automation

DON'T

LOSE SIGHT OF YOUR PURPOSE.

Too often, leaders jump into presentations with a catchy start, then fail to deliver on the ultimate goal. It's nice to grab the audience's attention, but you also need to keep it.

DO

START WITH THE GOAL IN MIND.

Even if it's an update for a group you see regularly, consider how you can maximize the opportunity to further your goals and accelerate the progress of whatever you are working on.

What do you need from this group? What type of information are you trying to gather or deliver? What feedback or insights would be beneficial to your project?

BE INFLEXIBLE.

If you're attached to the exact order and plans, you don't allow yourself to respond to the needs of the audience, which is the ultimate goal for any presentation.

BE PREPARED FOR ANYTHING.

Whether it's an internal or external audience, be ready to adapt your plan to accommodate shorter time frames and still meet your objectives.

Practice delivering the presentation in the allotted time, give the same presentation in half the time, and consider what you would say if you had only five minutes to capture the essence of your message. It will force you to be clear on the outcome you seek, the critical facts you need most and how you would create dialogue if you had less time.

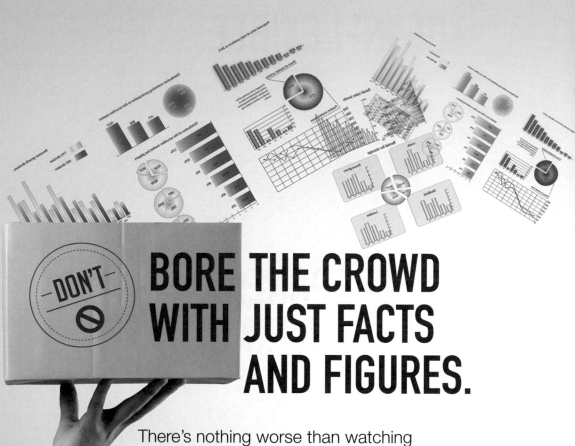

BORE THE CROWD WITH JUST FACTS AND FIGURES.

DON'T

There's nothing worse than watching the eyes glaze over as you present table upon table of numbers and facts on a PowerPoint slide.

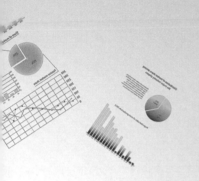

TELL A FULL STORY, WITH A BEGINNING, MIDDLE AND END.

I'm a huge believer in storytelling to capture an audience, and I preach it often with my clients. Yet it's amazing to me how resistant leaders can bo to storytelling in their presentations. As I say often, people remember stories, not facts and figures.

PRESENTATION LESSONS
FROM A PRO.

One of my favorite articles in *Harvard Business Review*[12] is from Chris Anderson, curator of TED. It's entitled "How to Give a Killer Presentation," and it draws from 30 years of learnings since the first TED conference. TED speakers have run the gamut from political figures, musicians and TV celebrities to less familiar figures from academia and scientific circles. Yet Anderson is convinced—as I am— that giving a good talk is highly coachable. He writes, "In a matter of hours, a speaker's content and delivery can be transformed from muddled to mesmerizing."

Among some of Anderson's most enlightening tips:

 Frame your story. "When I think about compelling presentations, I think about taking an audience on a journey. A successful talk is a little miracle—people see the world differently afterward."

 Don't put too much in. "If you try to cram in everything you know, you won't have time to include key details, and your talk will disappear into abstract language…" Limit the scope of your talk to that which can be explained, and brought to life with examples, in the available time."

Think like a detective. "Many of the best talks have a narrative story that loosely follows a detective story. The speaker starts out by presenting a problem and then describes the search for a solution. There's an 'aha' moment, and the audience's perspective shifts in a meaningful way."

Beware of the biggest mistakes. Number one mistake? Forgetting about the power of narrative. "If a talk fails, it's almost always because the speaker didn't frame it correctly, misjudged the audience's level of interest, or neglected to tell a story. Even if the topic is important, random pontification without narrative is always deeply unsatisfying."

Pay attention to your tone. "Some speakers may want to come across as authoritative or wise or powerful or passionate, but it's usually much better to just sound conversational. Don't force it. Don't orate. Just be you."

Hone your best stage presence. "There are some people who are able to walk around a stage during a presentation, and that's fine if it comes naturally. But the vast majority are better off standing still and relying on hand gestures for emphasis."

Make eye contact. "Perhaps the most important physical act onstage is making eye contact."

Handle nerves. Proven advice: simply breathe deeply.

Have something to say. "If you have something to say, you can build a great talk. But if the central theme isn't there, you're better off not speaking."

FEEL THAT YOUR ROLE DOESN'T REQUIRE YOU TO BE A STRONG PRESENTER.

We often hear from leaders who aren't convinced that good speaking skills really matter. They may be in an engineering or analytical role and feel that their contributions in those areas are more important than their ability to communicate or capture an audience.

Yet if you can't reach your teams on an emotional level, you've failed at one of the most important roles as a leader.

TAKE PRESENTATIONS SERIOUSLY.

The best leaders understand that presentations are a fantastic opportunity to drive a business forward — whether it's an external audience or a large group of your own employees.

Cisco Puts Executives' Presentation Skills On A Scorecard

A recent piece on leadership in *Forbes*[13] beautifully underscores the importance of presentation skills. It discusses former Cisco CEO John Chambers' "obsession" with improving the presentation and speaking skills of his executive teams. To ensure his team was working to be the best presenters they could be, every one of Cisco's executives were rated by the audience on their content and delivery after important presentations. This applied to customer presentations as well as speeches to employees.

Chambers strongly believes that a company can "move faster and execute faster if it communicates well internally," says communication coach and author Carmine Gallo, who wrote the *Forbes* article. Employees or customers were asked to give executives a score from 1 to 5 for two key points:

Delivery: The presentation was delivered clearly and effectively

Content: I understand how this solution/topic can be applied within my business

Forbes reported that Chambers also welcomed ratings of his own speeches and sincerely appreciated honest feedback.

WHAT'S THE BEST PIECE OF ADVICE YOU'VE RECEIVED IN YOUR CAREER

Advice:
Be biased towards action and confident of success.

Back Story: As a CPA, my initial career success depended on my technical expertise and analytical capabilities. As a leader, in managing and succeeding through others, decisions became less straightforward, with no clear right or wrong answers and I had to accept there will never be enough information to make a perfect decision. To be successful, I had to recognize that falling, stumbling, and occasionally getting your wind knocked out is part of the journey. Rather than hesitating to act until all facts are known or until a plan contemplating every potential contingency was perfectly developed, I became more biased towards action, and through experience, more assured in my ability to handle and overcome the inevitable bumps in the road.

And as a leader, I have learned the importance of conveying and instilling in my teams a genuine confidence in the certainty of future success, despite whatever harsh realities we may confront. A conviction that with the right focus and resources, nothing is impossible.

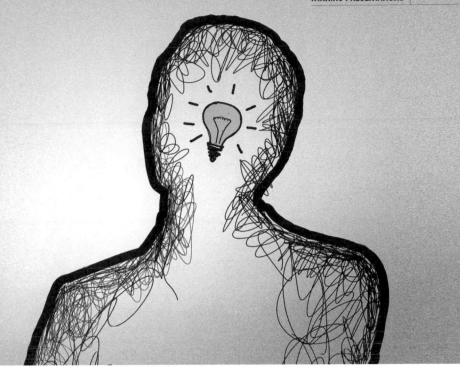

Outcome: Optimism is infectious. The inner courage as a leader to lean into challenges positively and optimistically, and the focus on together learning from mistakes and rebounding with renewed speed, conviction and confidence, have been crucial in motivating our teams and successfully driving us forward.

And for others, we show by example that cynics, victims, and fence sitters will be left behind.

Duane M. DesParte
Senior Vice President and
Corporate Controller, Exelon

CHAPTER SEVEN: Motivate and Inspire

What's the Story with Stories?

We all tell stories naturally that illustrate who we are as a person, what we do, and what we believe in. Think of your last conversation with a friend, someone in your family, or a neighbor at a barbecue. "Once upon a time" (or a spin on that) is a multiple-times-a-day occurrence.

Yet at work, something happens when we "badge in" at our organizations. Stories get lost, and pie charts and copy-heavy slides take over.

It's important to remember that we follow leaders because of how they make us feel. And stories are the most powerful way leaders can make an emotional connection with employees. Forget facts. Skip the supporting points. Push past the proof points. Stories rule.

This is especially true in many organizations where the majority of employees are left-brained, appreciate the literal, and value a logical sequence of facts. In these cultures, leaders aren't hardwired to share personal experiences, yet stories get the results other communications can't.

How powerful would it be if all leaders had a personalized storytelling platform with a library of stories that tie to the actions they need to accomplish? This kind of platform would help the leader find and raise his or her voice and drive the business results he or she wants.

Stories are the ultimate low-cost, high-return strategy. Isn't that what happily ever after is all about?

What will it take for you to codify your best stories into a library for you to use?

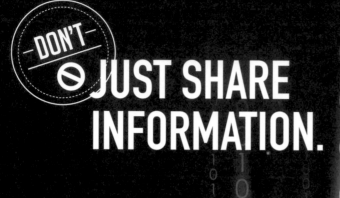

DON'T 🚫 JUST SHARE INFORMATION.

INFORMATION.

REMEMBER THAT LEADERSHIP IS ABOUT INSPIRATION.

At a recent leadership team meeting, a senior leader shared an insight that resonated incredibly well with the group. When discussing how to accelerate the organization's ability to deliver on their strategy, and the support leaders needed, he said: *"You provide the information, and I'll provide the inspiration."*

Now that's what I call leadership.

Here's what he knew (that every leader should know):

- **He's accountable** to communicate with his teams and to help them translate strategy into action—as a team and as individuals. He's not waiting for someone else—whether it's a member of senior leadership or the communications team—to do it for him.

- Organizations aren't great at inspiring people; **leaders inspire**. He's best equipped to motivate his people.

- Moving people to action takes **creating an emotional connection** with others. In this case, he realized the importance of painting a picture of the future and encouraging his team to join him. Facts and context are important, but it's tapping hearts that's most powerful and meaningful for employees.

If I could have given him a standing ovation, I would have. As it were, I already was standing, facilitating. Needless to say, I was beaming because I knew he got it. Then the CEO chimed in to reinforce this mindset and approach.

DON'T BE A DISTANT, UNKNOWN LEADER.

Employees don't want to follow leaders who they don't really know and understand. You can't get anywhere with your team if they don't see you as a real person who's not perfect but who has a real vision for the company.

HELP FOLKS GET TO KNOW YOU.

One of the key ways to help people get to know you is by sharing stories and connecting with employees on a personal level.

I often enjoy listening to commencement speeches for ideas on how leaders can successfully share personal anecdotes to inspire a team. One of my recent favorites was from Facebook Chief Operating Officer Sheryl Sandberg, who spoke to nearly 2,000 graduates of the City Colleges of Chicago.

One of the keys to Sandberg's speech is that it was full of stories, not boring statistics and data points. At the same time, all the narratives had a point that directly connected to her City College audience, made up of many minorities, immigrants and older students with families of their own.

Specifically, Sandberg shared accounts of her immigrant ancestors looking to build a new life in the U.S. She spoke of her grandfather's graduation from the City College of New York, and how that opened up new opportunities for future generations including Sandberg herself. She was also willing to be truly honest and vulnerable. She talked about mistakes on the job and lessons learned. She shared her insecurities growing up, the feelings of inadequacy she needed to conquer in order to succeed. These anecdotes prompt interesting questions for corporate leaders, too:

- **Which of your life experiences** can serve as inspiration for your employees?

- What can you share that makes you **vulnerable and relatable?** For example, what was your first career experience?

- What **mistakes** have you made that helped you become a **better leader?**

- Furthermore, what can you share that **personally connects** you to your company's vision and your team?

IGNORE THE POWER OF STORYTELLING.

Sometimes leaders dismiss stories because they feel unnecessary to them—too soft or off point. They may think, "My team just needs the facts!" However, a growing body of research proves that simply communicating facts won't accomplish your most important goal—moving people to action. Facts inform, but they don't inspire. There's power in storytelling, so don't ignore it!

TELL STORIES TO MOTIVATE YOUR TEAMS.

Neuroscientists and cognitive psychologists teach us that tapping people's emotions through storytelling clearly allows us to command an audience's attention.

For instance, the renowned cognitive psychologist Jerome Bruner's research finds that a fact wrapped in a story is 22 times more memorable. Michael Gazzaniga, another prominent psychologist at the University of California at Santa Barbara, argues that our conscious rational mind is always looking to attach meaning to events. When there is none, the mind invents meaning.

Many famous CEOs have used storytelling to solidify their own company narrative, as Sangeeeth Verghese explains in a *Forbes* article[14], "The CEO as Storyteller in Chief." He describes how Starbucks Chairman Howard Schultz often tells the story of his trip to Milan and his passion for the fresh, richly brewed expresso he discovered there and brought home with him. Schultz shares the story to emphasize with employees that their job goes well beyond selling coffee. It's truly about the passion for a quality experience, the kind of experience that has many of us standing in line daily for the opportunity to taste a Starbucks coffee.

Similarly, Bill Gates often talks about his early dream to put a personal computer on every desktop and in every home—at a time when the power and beauty of computers was still widely unknown. In fact, that dream enticed many business geniuses to join Gates in building Microsoft in its earliest days. That includes former Microsoft executive Steve Ballmer, who dropped out of business school to join the company while it was an unknown start-up searching for its future path.

Leading companies are picking up on the importance of storytelling and using narratives to drive their strategy.

Paul Smith, a consumer research executive and author of the book, *Lead with a Story: A Guide to Crafting Business Narratives that Captivate, Convince and Inspire*, shared some of his favorite examples of companies' storytelling with *Forbes* contributor Dan Schawbel[15]. Among them:

- All senior executives at Nike are designated corporate storytellers

- Bullet points were banned by 3M and replaced with a process of writing strategic narratives

- Kimberly-Clark has a 13-step program for crafting stories and giving presentations with them

- P&G hired Hollywood movie directors to teach its senior executives how to become better storytellers

- Some storytellers at Motorola belong to outside improvisational or theater groups to hone their story skills

DON'T ⊘ SEPARATE STRATEGY FROM YOUR STORIES.

While it's great to see leaders embrace stories, it's so important to realize that simply storytelling— without the goal of teaching employees what they need to do in their work—defeats your purpose.

DO ✓ USE STORIES TO CONNECT EMPLOYEES TO STRATEGY.

I've had several moments with clients when the power of storytelling really hits home with their teams. One recent experience stands out. It was one of those times when a light bulb clearly went on.

Two senior leaders I've been working with have realized the power of storytelling, and especially with those stories that help others get to know them better and see their passion for the company's strategy. One CEO was admittedly against sharing details about himself and his family.

"What does that have to do with business?" he asked one day.

"Everything," I said.

People want to know who you are before they will listen to what you have to say. And for new leaders, all stakeholders wonder, "Who is this person? And why should I believe and follow them?" With all the slides and facts and figures, charts and graphs, commitments, acronyms and videos, it's the stories that people remember and value.

On a recent town hall survey, about one-third of the comments focused on the CEO's personal comments. Employees used words like "refreshing" and commented that what she shared was "very different than what I thought I knew about her." Another said: "How refreshing to have some human element tossed in with business-speak."

And these weren't any old stories. They were stories with a purpose, and a strong connection to the needs of the business.

Hats off to these senior leaders for their willingness to be vulnerable and try something new. You can be sure that integrating stories into their communication is now a standard operating practice.

As those leaders saw, stories make executives human and relatable, and that's why it's important to use at least one story purposefully in every communication opportunity with other leaders and employees. It's smart to develop a customized repertoire of stories so that you have various personal stories for different messages that you want to communicate.

Examples of possible story plots include:

Dealing with change	Excellent performance
Leading our industry	Teamwork
Acting like a leader	My role at the company
Finding smarter processes	Discovery
Overcoming obstacles	Standing up for what you believe in
Making the most of a tough situation	Taking charge/leading

? WHAT'S THE BEST PIECE OF ADVICE YOU'VE RECEIVED IN YOUR CAREER

Advice:
Work in an industry that you have a personal passion for.

Back Story: I have always loved cars, so joining Aston Martin has been a real thrill for me. When I get up on Monday morning to go to work, I'm excited because I get to engage in a business I love.

We hear much talk about the car becoming less important, especially for the millennial generation. For me, so many great memories have been built around cars—traveling to a special destination, spending quality time with friends and family inside a great car; going to motor races and car shows. There are few products that can have such a profound influence.

Outcome: This passion for cars helps me as a manager, too, because I don't have to fake it. It's clear to everyone I work with that I love what I do, that I'm super engaged. I consider personal enthusiasm an important management advantage; one of the main challenges of leadership is motivation. More than anything else, you're looking for that key to inspire the hearts and minds of your team.

Doing my part to inspire the people I work with is exciting for me. I believe wholeheartedly in our vision to create extraordinary cars, and I take pride in being a part of this company. The potential for Aston Martin is significant, and I cherish the responsibility— together with the rest of the management team—of leading this company into its second century.

Simon Sproule
Director of Global Marketing and Communications, Aston Martin

DON'T ⊘ TELL STORIES WITHOUT A PURPOSE.

Sometimes leaders get so caught up with grabbing an audience's attention that they miss the point. For instance, a personal anecdote is great but only if it connects to what you're trying to communicate. In other words: It doesn't really matter if your son won the state high school basketball tournament unless his game-winning shot says something about what your company team needs to do every day.

DO ✓ INCLUDE A MORAL TO EVERY STORY.

I sum up this advice with leaders in a simple way: Wrap up your story with this comment: "I share this story because…" If you have a hard time with this statement, then your story doesn't have a moral, and thus shouldn't be shared with your team.

HERE'S A QUICK FORMULA TO TELL
THE BEST STORIES | 3 Cs + M

CONTEXT.
What was the situation?

CHARACTERS.
Who was involved?

MORAL:
What was the lesson
learned and how does it
apply to your employees?

CONFLICT.
What was the problem to be
solved or point of tension?

= YOUR STORY

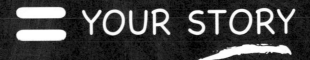

HOLLYWOOD'S TAKE ON STORYTELLING
FOR BUSINESS LEADERS.

In an often-cited piece for the *Harvard Business Review*[16], well-known Hollywood screenwriter and lecturer Robert McKee described just how much stories can elevate any leader's presentation from standard fare to the extraordinary.

"A big part of a CEO's job is to motivate people to reach certain goals. To do that, he or she must engage their emotions, and the key to their hearts is story," McKee told the *HBR*. "... If you can harness imagination and the principles of a well-told story, then you get people rising to their feet amid thunderous applause instead of yawning and ignoring you." He emphasized that audiences tend to forget lists and bullet points, but stories are "how we remember."

Importantly, McKee also emphasizes that leaders be truth tellers, not blind optimists. "Most companies and executives sweep the dirty laundry, the difficulties, the antagonists and the struggle under the carpet. They prefer to present a rosy—and boring—picture to the world. But as a storyteller, you want to position the problems in the foreground and then show how you've overcome them. When you tell the story of your struggles against the real antagonists, your audience sees you as an exciting, dynamic person. And I know that the storytelling works, because after I consulted with a dozen corporations whose principals told exciting stories to Wall Street, they all got their money."

Some other great narratives that leaders built stories from:

A CEO with a life-long love of doing puzzles talks about how that passion translates to the new business he's leading now. The job of transforming this Fortune 100 company requires everyone to be problem solvers, analytical thinkers, and completely focused on helping consumers with a complex set of needs.

A former track star who's now leading an organization through some tough challenges. He wants to be like his former sprinting coach, pushing the team to new lengths that they might feel are impossible. At the same time, this leader wants to understand when he can push and when he needs to back off a little and let his team breathe and grow.

KEY POINTS FOR
CRAFTING GREAT STORIES:

Stories are to:	An effective story should be:
Inspire, galvanize and engage	Simple, easy to tell, and easy to remember
Illustrate rather than assert. Stories accomplish the connections and results that abstract communication can't	Focused on a common goal or behavior
Create a sense of membership and unity through shared meaning	Purposeful and honest. Position the problems on the foreground and then show how they were overcome
Reach as many people as possible quickly. They can be easily retold to broaden the audience even further	Repeated. Keep telling your story until everyone is telling it

A leader who grew up in extreme poverty—surrounded by drugs and gangs—who now pulls from that tough early experience to understand the challenges faced by clients in the social service industry she works in.

An executive whose father was a family doctor who regularly made house calls. He talks about the fond memories he has of watching how responsive and caring his father was to patients' needs. Those memories keep him focused on what his health care organization should be all about: solving patient problems with sensitivity and selflessness.

STRATEGIC
STORYTELLING.

We've worked with scores of leaders over the years to help them craft stories from their personal lives that connect to the vision, mission and strategy of their organizations.

Here is one great example of a story a CEO developed to motivate his team.

> *My wife and I are remodeling a home we thought had great potential, but it needed more work than we originally thought; we needed to tear it down to the studs and rebuild. The whole experience reminds me of our work in a consumer-focused business. It was wonderful five years ago, but is now suffering from deferred maintenance. When we're done fixing it, we'll feel great because we're all in it together. I share this story because I want us to never give up on making our business better, no matter how hard it may seem today.*

CONTEXT: *My wife and I bought a house that needed remodeling. We knew it could be great.*

CHARACTERS: *My wife and I.*

CONFLICT: *The house turned out to need more remodeling than we expected.*

MORAL: *The whole experience reminds me of our work in a consumer-focused business. It was wonderful five years ago, but is now suffering from deferred maintenance. When we're done fixing it, we'll feel great because we're all in it together. I share this story because I want us to never give up on making our business better, no matter how hard it may seem today.*

DON'T ASSUME OTHERS KNOW YOUR INTENTIONS.

If you aren't clear about your intentions, people will start reading into them.

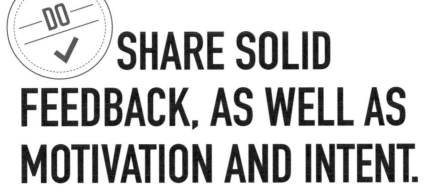

SHARE SOLID FEEDBACK, AS WELL AS MOTIVATION AND INTENT.

It seems like a simple communication point but many of us forget to share the motivations behind our actions. As a result, we can leave people scratching their heads.

Think about what grade you'd give yourself on how well you give employees feedback. Many of the executives I work with are brutally honest and give themselves an F. They don't make giving feedback a standard part of meetings and discussions; they give general ("good job!") versus specific feedback ("Here's what you did extremely well on this project…"); they often don't give feedback at all or wait too long to give feedback; and they would have a hard time giving their boss feedback.

The truth is most of us would be significantly more effective at work if we gave others feedback sooner and more regularly. It helps all of us work better. It helps us to recognize blind spots, know what to keep doing (and when to think about changing specific behaviors), and it helps build relationships with those who give us the gift of their advice.

Although we all might like to blame the challenges of giving feedback on external circumstances, the biggest barrier to giving feedback is often ourselves. It is difficult for most of us to offer criticism when we are looking someone in the eye. We're concerned about how a person will react. At the same time, we want to minimize conflict or protect our ego. Both lead to postponing the conversation or not having it at all.

Feedback is best given within a face-to-face context, as it is most likely to be well received and acted upon. When sitting down with an employee in person, we are better able to respond, coach, and teach to his or her defensiveness, to mitigate criticism with recognition of achievements, and to give someone time to absorb the message. There is simply no substitute for personal interaction when it comes to imparting honest feedback.

When you're ready to give feedback, timing matters. First, choose a time when you are at your best, and in the right frame of mind, so that there's the greatest chance that your comments will be heard, understood, and appreciated in the spirit that they're meant. Your credibility as a leader is at stake.

Once you're ready, ask the other person if they're open to hearing what you have to say. If so, proceed. If not, schedule a follow-up. Either way, offering a choice gets you off on the right foot (but don't let them off the hook if they're not ready; be persistent and let them know that you have an important message for them that affects how they work).

Once you pick the right time, here are the *"Four Fs of Feedback"* to help you move your grade from an *F* to an *A*:

FRAME

Set up the discussion and provide context as to why you're sharing feedback, including your motivation and intent. Most often, your intention is to be helpful, and it's critical to say that to establish a positive context for the discussion. State your motivation in a way that establishes the benefit to the listener. As you might expect, when employees are on the defensive, they are less likely to respond to and act on the comments. Here's what a good approach might sound like: "I need to share some feedback with you. My intention is for this to be helpful to you and for you—and us—to be more effective. If it were me, I would want to receive this feedback."

FEEDBACK

Discuss what went well or what could be better, and suggest an alternative. Feedback should never be personal; discuss a specific behavior and then the consequence. For example, "This behavior had this consequence, and here's what I'd prefer to see…" Avoid emotionally charged language or judgments, and just state the facts as they are.

OFTEN THE BIGGEST BARRIER TO GIVING FEEDBACK
IS OURSELVES.

Avoid emotionally charged language or judgments, and just state the facts as they are:

"I need to give you feedback…, here's my intention…, here's what I saw and the consequence…, here's what I'd prefer to see…, how do you feel?"

FEELINGS

Check to see how effectively you're communicating by creating a two-way dialogue. A simple "How do you feel about what I just said?" gives a person permission to respond and to share their impressions and understanding— and any context that you might not know about that might explain their behavior. Let them respond without interruption, then clarify or amplify if needed.

FOLLOW UP

Discuss specific next steps and how you can help. This is also your chance to help your staff understand that feedback has become an important part of your leadership style, and that you're fostering an environment in which it will become common. Make sure they understand feedback is a two-way street, and that you expect them to feel comfortable sharing it and other ideas in the spirit of continuous improvement. Of course, this means you must demonstrate the same behaviors when receiving feedback that you expect of your people when you give it.

Being timely and direct are essential for success. Add a little humanity and caring, and you have a recipe for successfully giving feedback that will build valued, trusting relationships.

DON'T

FORGET TO MATCH EMPLOYEE PASSION WITH WORK STREAMS.

DO

FIND OUT WHAT MOTIVATES YOUR EMPLOYEES AND KEEPS THEM ENGAGED.

Take in this sobering statistic: More than half the U.S. population now hates their job, according to researchers at the Conference Board[17]. This lack of employee engagement costs companies billions in productivity each year. Top employers know this, and they're convinced that engagement is no longer just about work-life balance or employees feeling good about their jobs. Instead, it's a key strategy for strengthening companies and building profits.

Still, what's less clear is how organizations can actually impact engagement. High performing companies realize that boosting employees' sense of commitment and passion for their work doesn't happen overnight. At the same time, they know that there are proven strategies for building an engaged, committed workforce— and that instilling a sense of passion into employees' work is one key way.

This isn't just about telling employees that they matter. It's about figuring out what employees want and need to do their jobs better, giving managers better tools for motivating their staffs, and aligning all employees around a shared purpose.

SIX STEPS TO HELP
EMPLOYEES GROW.

When you create a culture in which employees can reach their goals and know their thoughts and insights are appreciated, you boost productivity, morale, and engagement. Put these six tips into practice to help employees grow.

1. Encourage professional development. High-potential employees are not satisfied with the status quo. If given the proper guidance in their development, they will become the future leaders of your organization.

2. Create a development plan. Help your employees establish goals that are aligned with their strengths, interest and experience, as well as with the overall business strategy. Establish goals and expectations to help them set their sights on career opportunities.

3. Pair employees with mentors. Find someone who is in a similar role to the employee. Mentoring relationships can foster positive and productive working relationships, helping employees learn and gain encouragement and support in their careers. When coached with encouragement, your employees can help your business adapt to changes and reach the next level of success.

4. Help them build their networks. Recommend opportunities within the organization, as well as networking or professional groups that will help them build strong connections.

5. Challenge employees with assignments. Get your employees to leave their comfort zones. Employees can't move forward if they don't grow, and they can't grow if they never leave their comfort zones.

6. Show employees you trust them. If you want to help employees develop, trust them to do their jobs by getting out of the way. Let them know what your expectations are by modeling the behavior you expect—show them you trust them. This not only lets employees know what they need to succeed and gives them greater ownership, but it also shows them that credibility and trust are important in your organization.

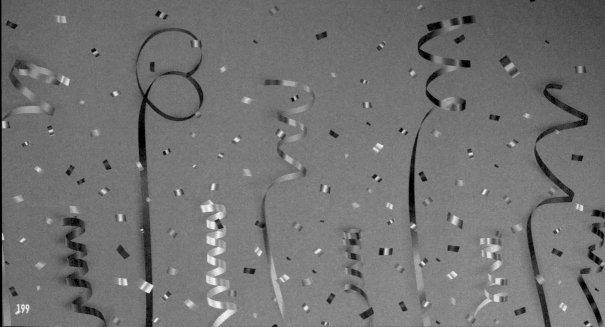

FORGET TO ACKNOWLEDGE YOUR EMPLOYEES' ACCOMPLISHMENTS.

Failing to recognize employees for a job well done is a classic leader mistake that leads to disengagement.

ALWAYS GIVE RECOGNITION.

It's a question I often get from leaders: "Do I need to praise someone on my team for 'just doing his or her job?'" My answer is always yes.

Jobs don't inspire and motivate people; leaders do. And leaders can easily fall into a trap where they question the logic of praising someone for doing what's expected of them. But recognition for a job well done is a top motivator for employees.

The best leaders know that the only way to get things done and move a business forward is through people. That means leaders need to go beyond lifting up employees who need extra motivation and recognize those who exhibit the behaviors you want to continue to see. Saying thank you for a job well done and rewarding employees who exhibit your desired behaviors seems simple, but it's often overlooked.

Here are a few simple yet powerful ways to share recognition with your team:

- **Match the reward to the person:** Start with individual preferences. Reward employees in ways they truly find rewarding

- **Match the reward to the achievement:** Effective reinforcement should be customized to take into account the significance of the achievement

- **Be timely and specific:** To be effective, rewards need to be given as soon as possible after the desired behavior or achievement. Being specific about what you appreciated will help create a culture of appreciation and encourage others to adopt similar behaviors

WHAT'S THE BEST PIECE OF ADVICE YOU'VE RECEIVED IN YOUR CAREER

Advice: *Work is personal.*

Back Story: When I started a new job several years ago, I was full of ideas and strategies to lead the team in moving from being a solid-performing organization to a best-in-class team. As I began full immersion into our new strategy I had to face a serious fact—we were not making progress. I had to take stock and realize that my hard-charging approach wasn't getting us anywhere. Then I remembered something my pastor said one Sunday: "People don't care about how much you know until they know how much you care."

Outcome: It hit me ... ***Work is personal***. Strong leaders understand this principle and practice it every day. I used to think that I could separate my authentic self between my "work" persona and my "home" persona. The reality is that people see right through it and if they think their leader isn't being real with them, they won't be real with their leader. Bring your whole self to the job and your colleagues will do the same. When that happens, the team's performance improves, and everyone wins.

Charlene A. Wheeless
Global Corporate Affairs,
Bechtel Corporation

CHAPTER EIGHT: Courageous Conversations at Difficult Times

A Personal Role Model For Courage.

I buried my mother at the end of 2012. I knew the day would come, yet it was way too soon. She had been diagnosed with leukemia, and the worst kind.

GG, as she was called, had two goals, and was uncharacteristically direct with her doctor the day she was diagnosed: "I have a grandchild coming (my second daughter), and a wedding to attend (her grandson's), and you're going to help me get there," she said, leaning her head close in to his and pointing at him. My mom abhorred pointing.

I thought to myself, "That's what I call determination."

I would come to find out how determined my mom could be.

I always thought I was a courageous person. Some day, I hope to have half the courage she had. The Yiddish word is chutzpah, which is defined as gall, brazen nerve, incredible guts. That fits Mom well.

How might the workplace be with a little more chutzpah? With more courageous conversations? I firmly believe there's more courage inside each of us than we might even think, and how powerful it would be to tap some of that—for our benefit and the benefit of others:

- To ensure senior leaders hear the truth, even when the news is bad
- To take the high road when a co-worker acts in a passive-aggressive way
- To be more direct in our feedback with others, because the people around us need feedback to be better
- To do what's right, even when it means ending a relationship or losing business

These are the actions that speak to the essence of who someone is. And many of us have these defining moments regularly.

The choice is ours. The easy path or the one that requires a little chutzpah?

In the words of my then 2½-year-old, "I promise to remember GG." Me, too. There's much to remember, and then there are the parts of her that are in me forever. These last lessons were some of the most powerful and important. And that's the greatest gift of all.

What actions can you take today to be a more courageous leader?

PANIC.

Too often in times of crisis, we rush
to communicate without thinking
through the best approach. It's better
to stop and think about how we
should handle the communications,
whether it's during a crisis or not!

HAVE MORE CALM, COURAGEOUS CONVERSATIONS.

If you were to commit to some additional chutzpah in your communications, then where might you focus your energies?

Here are ways to build more courageous conversations:

1. Have the tough conversations that you've been meaning to have. Many of us have important thoughts that remain unsaid—conversations that would be valuable to have. Addressing issues upfront is the only way to keep everyday speed bumps from mushrooming into larger problems. Tell people what they need to hear—not what they want to hear. It's often through tough conversations that we build relationships and cement bonds.

2. Stop talking and listen more. We know what we personally think. The real opportunity is in knowing what others think. People act to support their best interests, so we need to understand where they're coming from. The more you know about how someone else thinks, the easier it will be to persuade and move them to action. The answer: Stop talking. Literally. The most effective leaders spend the majority of their time observing, asking questions, absorbing and listening. Research on difficult negotiations reveals that the party who wins is usually the one who speaks the least. Why? They're gathering information that is incredibly helpful to them in planning their next move.

3. Pick up the phone or walk down the hall to actually talk with someone. Don't let email, instant messaging and other electronic forms of communication be a barrier to human interaction. Challenge yourself to pick up the phone two more times each day, especially if you have staff who work remotely. If you can't find the time to walk the halls, then schedule an appointment for yourself to do it.

4. Ask for what you need to succeed. To get what you want—in life or in work—you have to be able to articulate your needs and advocate for yourself in a positive way. When a deadline is unrealistic, do you ask for time to do quality work? When you're missing background information on a project, do you politely insist on a briefing before you begin work? It might be easier to remain silent, but being assertive shows that you respect yourself and others.

5. Communicate bad news in the same way, and with the same zest, as good news. It's easy to communicate when times are good, or when you have good news to share. When the news is bad, the tendency is often to wait to communicate, or to not communicate at all. You might feel like if you don't talk about it, then it doesn't exist. While you're waiting to communicate, the information vacuum fills. It's human nature to make interpretations— whether right or wrong—in the absence of information. Tell employees what you know, when you know it. That's all they expect.

6. Ask for feedback. Everyone needs feedback. Learn to say the following: "I'm continually working on how to lead better and would appreciate your feedback. Can you give me one skill that I do well and one area where I can be even better?" Listen carefully, ask questions and thank the person for his or her perspective. Resist the urge to be defensive, which will surely prevent you from receiving honest feedback in the future.

If people can't think of something in the moment, then don't let them off the hook. Suggest that you will follow up with them and then do it. Take your feedback to heart and commit to trying some of the ideas suggested. And, if the feedback is working, then loop back with the person who suggested it, and thank them.

7. Work on your blind spot. We all have blind spots. In our personal lives, our spouses or best friends tell us what we need to hear, and they know us better than we know ourselves in some ways. Likewise, we have blind spots in how we lead. Ensure that you have a "truth teller" or two at work who can help you when you get in your own way and don't realize it.

8. Embrace employees as decision makers. Tap your people to help you plan and solve problems. Chances are the people closest to a problem already have ideas about how to resolve the issue. Employees support what they help create. Ask and involve them.

9. Don't forget the fundamentals. Always speak the truth, without exception. Share the big picture first. It helps for everyone to start with the same base of knowledge. Cover the basic questions that employees have first—who, what, where, when, why and how. Say please and thank you. Constantly communicate the "why" to make action meaningful. Always answer the question, "What's in it for me?" and "Why should I care?" Tell people what they need to do and help them do it. Ask questions so that you hear employees' opinions. If you don't know the answer, then say so.

Executing on these top points takes courage and speaks to the essence of the kind of leader you are. The choice is yours:

The easy path or the one that requires a little chutzpah.

Let's not wait. We have everything that we need right now to succeed, including all of the courage needed to lead in a compassionate, productive and healthy way.

? WHAT'S THE BEST PIECE OF ADVICE YOU'VE RECEIVED IN YOUR CAREER

Advice:
Invest effort into helping people—we have to allow others to win before we can win.

Back Story: I was working for my father's trucking company early in my career, and I wasn't happy. I felt like a failure, stuck in the family business with no place to go. The longer I worked there, the less intelligent everyone seemed. I was unable to appreciate the people around me. They weren't as educated as I was and I thought I knew more than they did. I seemed mean or angry all the time. No one really wanted anything to do with me.

One day my father asked me why I was so difficult. "Why don't you invest a little effort into helping people?" he told me. "You should give people a reason to like you. You are a naturally likeable guy, but you've been a real jerk lately. People do a better job if they like being around you than they'll ever do for a mean, angry, sour-puss. You could be so much better if you weren't so hard to be around." I had recently become a Christian and Dad's advice really struck a chord. My goal had been to get everyone to do what I wanted but then I thought about what would happen if I actually focused on others and not on myself?

Outcome: Over time, I became more aware of my attitude and I wasn't very proud of it. Because of Dad's advice (or criticism) and my new understanding of my purpose and my faith, I adopted a new goal: to know and help the people around me. I developed a genuine interest and concern for others. Over time, I realized everyone else wasn't "unintelligent" but rather they had a different perspective on things. Sometimes their perspective was better than mine, and sometimes we informed each other. Once I started seeing others as valuable people, work became more enjoyable, and I became more influential. Once I started helping everyone else be successful in their job, I saw that their success determined the success of the company—and of my job too.

Years later, I heard the leadership coach and writer John C. Maxwell say, "People don't care how much you know until they know how much you care." Every job since then, I've tried to serve the people around me, making them successful and helping them in any way I can. The person who brings grace and a smile into a situation is always contagious, and there is influence, growth and achievement for all. We have to allow others to win before we can win. I'm grateful to my dad for investing in me and having the painful conversation that made the biggest difference in my leadership and career.

Mike Henry Sr.
Vice President,
Information Technology,
SageNet LLC

WAIT TO COMMUNICATE UNTIL YOU HAVE ALL THE ANSWERS.

-DON'T-

You want to wait to communicate. Until you have more information. Until you have "all the answers."

Until it's often too late.

Employees think about worse-case scenarios. They invent facts. They make things up. Worse yet, what employees surmise is happening in their minds usually is much worse than the planned change. And, if you wait, chances are that you're going to have to do clean up, which is inefficient and takes significant time.

" The information vacuum fills whether we want it to or not. And most often, it's filled with negative thoughts.

COMMUNICATE WHAT YOU KNOW.

Three of the most credibility-enhancing words for leaders are, *"I don't know."*

Employees know you're not omnipotent and realize that in some cases, you don't have the answers yourself. It's better to say you don't know than open your mouth and make it obvious you don't know by your long and winding answer.

On the other hand, chances are you have at least information that would be valuable to employees and merits communication to them. Here's what employees would tell you about their needs during times of change:

- Tell me what you know today. I understand when you don't have all the facts or details

- Keep me in the loop as plans develop. I want to know what you know when you know it

- Tell it to me straight. I'm an adult and can handle tough news. I might not like what you share but I will respect you for being direct with me and helping me understand what's happening

Think 3 + 1.

1. What we know

2. What we don't know

3. What we're working on figuring out

+

Proactively bust myths and facts you're hearing

Think you're not ready to communicate?

List possible answers to 3 + 1 and see whether there's enough information employees would find valuable to merit communication.

In almost all cases, you'll have enough information, and begin an all-important dialogue that will help you minimize the downside of change and maximize the upside.

DON'T USE SPIN.

Telling people what you think they want to hear erodes trust.

DO BE TRANSPARENT AND HONEST.

Employees are adults and they can handle the truth. Tell them what they need to hear in a direct and compassionate way. The fact is, they may already know the truth, and it's a relationship builder and shows you care.

EMPHASIZE THE NEGATIVES.

While it's important to be honest, negativity can quickly drag down even the most optimistic of teams. People want a reason for hope and a path for recovering from a tough situation.

CHANGE YOUR APPROACH TO CONVERSATIONS.

If you change the way you talk about things, the things you talk about will change.

You often can resolve a negative situation by changing the context and your delivery. Your words and actions set the tone for those who follow you and your lead:

- Paint the picture of what's possible: help people imagine and live the success you're aiming for

- Think about the way you have been talking about a major initiative or project. Is it positive? Hopeful? Filled with energy? Cautious? Fearful? Doubtful? Rethink your delivery to inspire and uplift your team

- Are you celebrating the early wins and successes?

If your approach to discussing business results leaves people feeling less than enthused, change your approach to a team-inspiring one, and watch the results change.

DON'T IGNORE THE GRAPEVINE.

Some call it the grapevine; others call it hearsay. No matter what you call it, it can be problematic and distracting. If you aren't talking proactively about issues that are important to your employees, chances are that someone else is.

TALK TO YOUR MANAGERS WHEN EMPLOYEES ARE BUZZING ABOUT A CRISIS.

All organizations have a rumor mill. It's a natural part of the employee network. And as much as leaders would like to shut it down, they can't. But they can manage it.

Five easy strategies for managing the company rumor mill:

1. **Maintain your credibility and use it to your advantage.** Credibility won't stop rumors from developing, but it will unleash the truth. It's about communicating what you know, when you know it, and make sure your messages are consistent across all touch points.

2. **Be open, but be careful.** We know that remaining silent in tough times feeds anxiety and fuels the rumor mill. But being too open can hurt more than it helps, especially if it adds to people's fears.

3. **Pulse your people.** Ask your direct reports what they're hearing from their people on a periodic basis. Or, better yet, walk the halls and ask employees what's on their minds. Having a better sense for what keeps employees up at night will help you get ahead of any rumors that might be waiting in the wings. The best part is that employees will know you're listening and that you care about what they are thinking.

4. **Anticipate and address concerns.** When people are worried about what they don't know, they often imagine the worst and share their concerns with others. If leaders don't anticipate and address concerns, the vacuum will fill with rumors. Get out in front of anticipated worries by understanding the mindset that causes them and immediately address those concerns.

5. **Include your own messages in the rumor mill.** Engage thought leaders who typically feed and influence the rumor mill, along with supervisors throughout the organization. When employees hear the same messages from their supervisor (always their preferred source) or from the CEO, read it on the internet, and hear it through the rumor mill, they're more likely to believe it and, most importantly, act on it.

PHRASES TO HELP LEADERS SHARE
WHAT THEY KNOW.

I don't know that, but what I can tell you is...

No, let me explain...

That's the way it used to be. Here's what we do now...

As I know more, I'll update you...

TUMULTUOUS TIMES CALL FOR MORE
COMMUNICATION
AND COURAGE.

In times of change or uncertainty, organizations need leadership more than ever. That means the quality and amount of communications needs to increase. Times of change are a litmus test for leadership, which means sharing with employees what we know and what we don't know.

A COURAGEOUS COMMUNICATOR
CHALLENGE.

Think of information that you are consciously withholding from your team. But instead of holding back, share a) what you know and b) what you don't know. Then begin a dialogue with your team about the information and how to understand it.

DON'T

AVOID CONFLICT.

It's a paradox that every leader faces: Create teams that work well together but embrace conflict. Also, drive consensus but encourage individual points of view. Discomfort is emotional. Feelings can be complex and multi-layered. But stifling expression can inhibit a team's performance and lead to poor decision-making.

EMBRACE CONFLICT.

It's a given: Having tough conversations and communicating difficult topics is part of a leader's job. But just like you plan for contingencies in your business, planning how you will communicate difficult messages can improve the ultimate outcome. It is seldom easy to share difficult news, but thinking through your approach in advance definitely can improve the process.

It's human nature to avoid conflict; we're wired in that way. I was talking with a leader recently about conflict and how he avoided it, which he acknowledged cost him time, energy, and negatively impacted relationships with others.

The principle I share with leaders who avoid conflict is simply this: go toward the conflict. Our natural tendency is to move away from it and avoid it. It's only through what might feel like "rupture" that "repair" can happen. That's the upside of conflict handled well—improved relationships and trust.

Handling tough conversations involves two aspects: crafting a clear message and having the conversation.

HERE ARE SIX STEPS
TO PREPARE:

STEP 1:

STEP 2:

Identify the problem.

What's the issue in the business? How are your results affected? Are there undesired behaviors that need to change?

Identify your desired outcome.

What is your objective for the conversation? Are you trying to put business news in context for your employees? Do you need your team to understand changes that are under way? Do you need desired behaviors to become the norm among your staff?

STEP 3:

Identify your audience.

Who needs to hear this information? Do you need to inform your entire staff? Is it a small group? Is it one employee? And should they all hear the message at the same time, or should some people hear it before others?

What do you want your audience(s) to think, feel and/or do?

- Consider how they might feel and receive the information you want to share.
- What concerns might they have and what perspective might they have?
- What are their needs and fears? Do you share common concerns?
- How have you or they contributed to the problem and what would help it improve?

STEP 4:

Structure your key messages/conversation.

What will you say to employees in a calm, constructive way so they understand the situation and your concerns?

- Consider how to start the conversation.
- Develop specific messages or even a script to deliver the key points.
- Identify the questions you will ask (to seek input/check for understanding). For example, "Tell me how you feel about what I just said."
- Have stories or examples to share to illustrate your main point.
- Outline specific actions being taken and/or that your employees need to take.

STEP 5:

STEP 6:

Deliver your message.

When it is time to deliver the message, select the right time and place to have a conversation with privacy and without distraction. Encourage dialogue so you can get real-time insight on how employees are receiving the information, what's on their minds, and if they understand what you are saying. Allow for plenty of time to be sure they feel supported and listened to.

Follow up.

Be sure to make yourself available to answer questions—in front of a group as well as privately. Ask what's on their minds and listen with empathy to people's concerns. Confirm next steps or expectations and timeline for completion, including any commitments you make to follow up on their expressed concerns.

CHAPTER NINE: Email Etiquette Guide

Why Online Manners Elude Us.

Emily Post published the ultimate guide to social interactions, *Etiquette*, in 1922. The book quickly became a bestseller and is now in its 18th edition. Clearly, the desire for social guidance is undiminished. Thanks to Post, many of us at least know the right thing to do in most social situations. Whether we always do it is another story.

Yet when it comes to the technology frontier, many of us frequently behave badly. That's not because we mean to be rude, but because we struggle with good manners in our virtual communications. Since we first started communicating via email in the mid-90s, much has improved: The Wild-West, anything-goes mentality of early email has been replaced, in many cases, by self-censoring based on lessons learned the hard way about how to use—and not use—email.

But when it comes down to it, many of us are still in the dark about the manners and rules that define good email. Why? The answer is simple: We haven't had much guidance on the dos and don'ts. Nowhere is all of this more apparent—and more frustrating—than in the workplace. It's where emails fly back and forth all day, every day. This endless stream of communication contains valuable information, but there's so much noise. So much clutter. And it takes so much of our time.

An important question when it comes to productivity is this: *Which of your bad habits—if you were able to fix them—would help you be more effective at work?*

By having employees ask this key question, organizations can introduce their teams to an entirely new approach to email. In some cases, employees have made a personal commitment or pledge—to get better at their email communication, using some critical tips.

The encouraging news is that many companies I've worked with have seen great results—and higher productivity—after spending more time focusing on better email practices.

CAN YOU SEE YOURSELF IN THESE

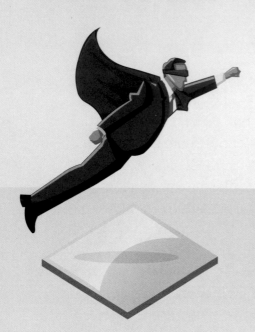

Captain No-Context

Bombards recipients with emails that lack a clear point and any necessary background. The Captain is on a mission to the land of ambiguity, leaving others behind and confused. If only the Captain would consider the real goal and keep the message concise, everyone would get to the destination faster.

Drama Queen

Excitement abounds in the Queen's emails that are often full of TOO MANY capital letters, exclamation points, emoticons or abbreviations. The Drama Queen needs to remember their audience will respond better when they're courteous and professional in their correspondence—a business email is not a text message. ☺

TROUBLED EMAIL CHARACTERS?

The Gunslinger

Charges into the wide open *Wild West*—a rebel without a clue— and fires off large group emails. He also responds by hitting "reply-all," instead of considering who really needs the message. Whoa Nelly! It's time to pull in the reins and determine the best fellow travelers.

The Hermit

Doesn't lift her head up from the screen and sometimes forgets that a phone call or face-to-face conversation could produce more mutual understanding, long-term relationships, and outcomes.

The truth is we are all guilty of some email goofs and missteps from time to time. However, it's important to create a professional email persona that matches your personality and presence. The tips in this chapter can help you get there.

USE EMAIL TO HIDE.

Don't use email to avoid a difficult situation. Research shows us that conflict on email escalates faster and lasts longer.

CONSIDER HOW BEST TO COMMUNICATE.

An important first step to bringing order and civility to email culture is recognizing that email is not the only solution.

Think of all the great work that happens through personal interactions. When email becomes simply one of many communication choices, you'll naturally begin to use it more productively, relevantly, and politely. With this in mind, here's one simple fix: Keep in mind that email is never a substitute for a conversation, even if it's a quick one.

A further way to ensure that you're using email correctly is to think about your desired outcome before you start an email. What are you trying to accomplish? Then, consider the alternatives. Would a different action get you to the outcome faster or more efficiently? Would a five-minute phone call or face-to-face discussion allow you to accelerate the project further, faster?

Choosing The Right Form Of Communication

What Email Is Good For:

- Informing others of a decision/ achievement/event
- Recapping action items
- Scheduling meetings
- Setting expectations
- Setting timelines
- Distributing written confirmation of previously discussed information
- Sharing documents or pre-read materials

What Email Is Not Good For:

- Conflict resolution
- Decision-making (unless it's easy)
- Presenting complicated information to achieve understanding and alignment
- Explaining changes or redirections that have immediate or direct implications for how someone needs to execute their work
- Tough conversations

IGNORE YOUR ROLE IN EMAIL OVERLOAD.

It's easy to think email overload is caused by someone else, but the truth is leaders are often the leading offenders of email overload. Don't dismiss your role in the problem!

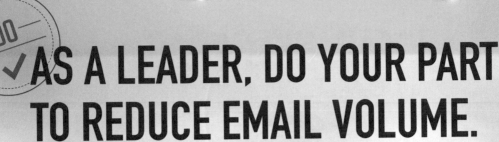

✓AS A LEADER, DO YOUR PART TO REDUCE EMAIL VOLUME.

Leaders set the tone for so much of what goes on in an organization—in both good and bad ways— and email use is certainly no exception.

Consider the experience of the London-based company International Power, which was featured in the September 2013 issue of the *Harvard Business Review*. The firm's seven-person management team wanted to increase efficiency and initially figured there was a problem with too many lower-level employees sending emails. Instead, the managers were shocked to learn from a detailed analysis that they personally sent an average of 56 messages per day.

Instead of looking to technology-based email management tools, the company's executive team tried reducing the number of messages they sent. The executives were trained to reduce email output by not forwarding as many emails, limiting the number of recipients, and using other forms of communication more often. The leaders then received weekly reports highlighting their progress.

According to HBR, the team's total email output dropped by **54 percent** as a result of the initiative. The 73 other London-based employees followed suit, also reducing their email messages, even without training. The overall result was an annual gain of 10,400 work hours, translating to a 7 percent increase in productivity. As a result of that experience, HBR suggested that companies can significantly reduce email volume by simply turning to the management team.

They suggested three key tips:

• Teach executives to be more deliberate in their e-mail use

• Ask executives to set a target for reducing the number of messages they send, and include it in their performance goals

• Give executives weekly feedback

EMAIL OVERLOAD
AT A GLANCE:[18]

THE AVERAGE
KNOWLEDGE
WORKER
SPENDS

28%

OF HIS OR HER WORK
WEEK **MANAGING EMAIL.**

JUST ONE HOUR OF NON-VALUED
ADDED EMAIL AMOUNTS TO

 **$500,000**

IN LOST REVENUE PER DAY AND
$240 MILLION IN LOST REVENUE
PER YEAR AT A COMPANY OF
NEARLY 50,000 EMPLOYEES.

THE AVERAGE
EXECUTIVE
OR MANAGER
LOGS IN

72 HOURS

ON A TYPICAL WORK
WEEK, LARGELY BECAUSE
OF THE ABILITY TO
CONNECT ONLINE AT
ANY TIME OF DAY.

TIPS FOR CHOOSING THE RIGHT
COMMUNICATION TOOLS

Face-to-face meetings are good to:

- Enable two-way communication to reach alignment and clarity on complex issues
- Build relationships
- Bring multiple points of view or project streams together at once
- Create new ideas/brainstorm
- Introduce new concepts and provide higher levels of context and background
- Discuss tough or sensitive topics
- Expedite decision-making

Phone or voicemail is good to:

- Initiate a request for a complex conversation—to provide the rationale for why the face-to-face meeting is necessary
- Provide a kind reminder about an impending or passed deadline
- Demonstrate the issue (or person) at hand is a priority
- Enable the audience to hear emotion in your voice (urgency, pleasure, concern)

Instant messaging is good to:

- Ask a very brief or quick question
- Determine whether the person you would like to reach is available for a more detailed conversation (voice-to-voice or face-to-face)

Social collaboration tools are good to:

- Ask a large group for their input or feedback
- Crowdsource ideas
- Work together on a project or deliverable
- Build relationships among remote or virtual teams

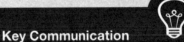

Key Communication Options To Consider:

- In-person conversations
- Group meetings
- Small group face-to-face meetings with supervisors, colleagues, leaders, etc.
- Phone call or voicemail
- Instant messaging (IM)
- Social collaboration tools (e.g., Yammer and Chatter)

DON'T

⊘ **FORGET TO TRAIN YOUR TEAMS ON HOW TO USE EMAIL.**

You can't assume everyone knows the key ways to reduce email volume. If they did, there wouldn't be so many darn emails.

DO

✓ **REINFORCE KEY EMAIL BEHAVIORS FOR YOUR TEAMS.**

Through communication campaigns and regular reminders, you can significantly reduce email volume simply by putting email overload on the agenda.

In some cases, an email "etiquette guide" can be helpful to identify the most common employee behaviors that drive up email volume and then offer solutions for addressing those blunders. Some of our clients have also introduced email "pledges" to help employees understand what they could do differently to dramatically reduce email volume.

BE LONG-WINDED.

A long email without a purpose is both unprofessional and risks sharing information that won't get read.

KEEP IT BRIEF.

Edit unnecessary words and use short sentences. If the subject requires some detail, use bulleted lists or bold important items to make the information easily digestible for the receiver.

The bottom line is we all need to practice clarity and concision when writing emails. The best emails aren't short narratives. Instead, it is more effective to simply alert people of key news and direct them to detailed information elsewhere.

LET A BAD EMAIL STRING BLOOM.

Don't be that person who just keeps piling on to the email string when the communication steers way off task or in a thousand new directions.

TAKE CONTROL OF EMAIL CONVERSATIONS.

It should go without saying that when it comes to sending emails, much of the burden for making good decisions and being mannerly ***falls on the individual sender.***

As soon as you see email strings getting out of control, jump in fast. A back-and-forth of more than three emails is a good indicator that a phone call or face-to-face meeting is necessary. Pick up the phone and call the original sender to clear up any misunderstandings. When you get an email that should have been a phone call, call the person and explain why.

It's also important to always answer all questions. One of the biggest reasons for long back-and-forth chains of emails is the person who only addresses two of the five questions posed. The result is that the sender has to follow up and ask the other three questions again. Avoid this frustration by answering each question asked—even if the answer is "I don't know, but I'll find out."

DON'T ⊘ CHECK EMAIL BY THE MINUTE.

If you're spending a lot of time responding
to every email that pops into your inbox,
chances are you're getting nothing done
other than reading email.

PICK SPECIFIC TIMES TO CHECK EMAIL.

If you set time limits on when you'll check email or specify certain times of the day that you'll log in, you can be much more efficient plowing through your other work without distractions.

In an interview with *Fortune*[19], Peter Bregman, author of *18 Minutes: Find Your Focus, Master Distraction, and Get the Right Things Done*, noted that there's a reason email checking has gotten out of control. "Email is such a seductress in terms of distraction because it poses as valid work," he told *Fortune*.

 If you could get away with watching TV, you probably would…but you probably can't, so instead you check email."

To combat this problem, Bregman advised checking email three specific times per day. If you need to check email more regularly, another option is to read it just once per hour, and set a limit on how much time you'll spend per hour.

EFFECTIVELY MANAGING
TIME ON EMAIL:

As a sender, plan ahead:

- Give colleagues a heads up if you may need help on something pressing outside of business hours

- For truly urgent emails, reach out via phone, instant messenger or text message to let your colleague know about the email

- Refrain from emailing someone on vacation unless you've gotten prior approval from them. Reach out to the colleague covering for them instead

When to hit send to manage perceptions of urgency:

- Time your emails to make them most effective: You can help manage the perception of urgency or expectation by choosing an appropriate time to send your message and anticipating the reaction of the recipient

- If you're working at odd hours to accommodate your own schedule, consider saving emails in your draft folder to be sent at a later time

- You can also schedule delivery times for emails by selecting "delay delivery" under the Options tab and setting the day/time you want your message sent

- If you lead a team that needs to be engaged after hours or on weekends, set clear expectations about availability and responding to email during those times to address business needs

-DON'T- THINK ONE SIZE FITS ALL.

When it comes to email, no two people prefer the same thing.

—DO— KNOW THE HABITS OF YOUR EMAIL RECIPIENTS.

Tailor the tone, style and organization of information included in your message to meet the needs of your audience. If you do not know the recipient well, it's best to play on the safe side by writing a more formal, yet concise, email.

Think about the five people who you most frequently email—chances are one has distinct preferences for how they like to receive information, the appropriate tone they expect and a suitable response time window. For example, you may learn that your boss prefers to read email first thing each morning so it is best to send any important news or updates pertaining to that day's work in advance. Getting to know your top email recipients' preferences and habits will ensure smooth communications.

CREATE A FALSE SENSE OF URGENCY WITH EMAIL.

This means senders should not expect a response to emails outside a colleague's normal business hours. Avoid sending emails to colleagues on vacation unless the matter is urgent or the sender had previously arranged to send critical information. Some of the worst email behavior takes place when senders fail to respect a colleague's time.

RESPECT WORK-LIFE BOUNDARIES.

One of the harsh realities of email is it allows us to reach anyone at any time. As a result, many employees are feeling overwhelmed by the growing volume of emails they receive every day. This causes "expectation stress," or the feeling that employees are expected to be available "24/7."

Employees want to reclaim their personal lives—and they aren't shy anymore about telling their employers what they want. Smart employers are heeding the message, as research shows that employees who have balance in their lives are actually more productive at work.

To respect colleagues' commitments, consider the following key behaviors:

- If your need is urgent, consider a phone call or instant message instead
- Appreciate that colleagues may be engaged in other high-priority work or meeting with customers, traveling, or on PTO
- Allow more time for responses if it's a holiday or weekend, unless you've gained prior agreement about a colleague's availability
- In general, 24 to 48 hours is a standard response time for non-urgent business

DON'T LET YOUR INBOX GET BEYOND ONE SCROLL.

Try to not let your inbox pile up or it will be nearly impossible to find important information that needs responding/action after one day. Clear out new emails daily or set aside time on Friday for cleaning. The rule of thumb is that your entire inbox list should not exceed one scroll of the mouse.

DO GET ORGANIZED.

The first step to managing your email is getting organized and creating a system that works just for you. Consider creating folders for different projects and filing emails as they come in. Create rules for frequent emails that come in the form of news alerts. Subscription based emails can be sent directly to dedicated folders and bypass your inbox.

STAND SILENT.

If you're getting unwanted emails, it's important to speak up.

GIVE FEEDBACK ON POOR COMMUNICATION.

Let colleagues know how you feel about receiving unwanted email and ask them to limit similar activity in the future. If you're able to receive personal emails at work, ask friends to send them to your personal email account instead.

DON'T
BE FLIPPANT IN YOUR EMAIL RESPONSES.

When responding to an email, especially one regarding a serious or pressing situation, make sure you spell out clearly the next steps involved.

DO
BE PROFESSIONAL AND POLITE IN EMAIL.

Email may be informal but should never be sloppy, inaccurate or rude. Use correct grammar and spelling (no texting shortcuts) and be careful to use a positive tone so your communication is not misinterpreted.

KEY TIPS FOR BEING PROFESSIONAL
WITH EMAIL:

- **Begin all emails with salutations.** Launching straight into a message without a greeting can be off-putting. Keep it positive and collegial.

- **Avoid private or confidential conversations over email, if at all possible.** Once you send an email, it's out of your hands and can be forwarded along. Would you be comfortable with your message being seen by others? If not, consider whether email is the correct communication vehicle.

- **Never send an email when you're angry.** Once you hit the send button, it's not coming back and you can't take back what you said. If you're upset, get up, take a deep breath and really think about how you'll best handle the situation and what mode of communication would be most effective.

- **Use the high priority feature sparingly.** Be realistic about the urgency of your email. If too many of your emails carry a "high priority" flag, nothing you say will be viewed as a priority by anyone. Consider using a brief but descriptive subject line to note the topic and immediacy (if it exists).

- **Avoid sarcasm or tongue-in-cheek humor.** Written forms of communication, like email, aren't able to convey tone. The actual meaning behind sarcastic statements is often lost, resulting in confusion, frustration and poor morale.

- **Don't overuse the exclamation point.** Doing so can diminish the weight of your message and make you look unprofessional. Depending on how it's being used, it can also come across as shouting.

- **Don't try to recall a message.** Once the email has left your outbox, there's no turning back. Recalling a message won't prevent everyone from seeing it and may only attract more attention to the email. It's better to be deliberate and concise with your email content as you write it and check everything twice before sending.

- **Be timely.** Respond in a timely manner, if even to acknowledge that you received the message and are working on getting an answer to the person's question.

- **Give the meeting or conference call host a heads up** beforehand if you are expecting an important notice during a meeting so the host will understand why your attention may be diverted by email.

for e... ...te. Evening
and weekend hours available. Fax
application Attn: HR Dept.

Apply Today!

...ed
ate
...ne.
...c job.
...474
...ing.
...m

...re
...ed
...ne
...f.
...ng
...ses.
...octors,
...ided for
...ital Care
...staff ...M-F
...n to...
...re.com
...6975
...ay!
...$$

Y...
Nex...

TRAIN FO...

Informatio...
program...
today's ...
additiona...
may be r...
certain p...
Call Tod...

W...

Are y...
We a...
for s...
team...
Great...
Start...

★ N...

Caree...
Excitin...
oppo...
now...

• **Sales Reps Wanted**

Self Starter with 3 Yr. Sales Exp.
Necessary! Must have commercial

253

REPLACE MASS INTERNAL EMAILS WITH OTHER FORMS OF COMMUNICATION.

A number of researchers have suggested ways to diversify your communications. One suggestion that has worked for some is an electronic newsletter for various departments. This could be accessed online through the intranet or a SharePoint site, and employees can quickly narrow in on key information that's stored in one easily accessible spot.

Another option is to consider turning group email conversations into online discussion forums, much like a Facebook or LinkedIn chat.

Consider creating a customized company or team mobile app through YAPP, which can be helpful for sharing urgent news or important updates with large employee groups that include virtual and/or non-wired employees.

WHAT'S THE BEST PIECE OF ADVICE YOU'VE RECEIVED IN YOUR CAREER

Advice:
Never reach a stage in your career where you no longer spend a portion of your time writing (press releases, speeches, strategy, etc).

Back Story: One of my most influential mentors shared this with me during a development conversation. The intent here is that no matter how far your career takes you, be sure to always stay grounded in the core value that you provide. For a senior communicator, this means avoiding the bureaucracy and "politics" of an executive role where possible, to stay true to the core value of a top communications leader—delivering thoughtful solutions to drive business outcomes. It is an all-too-common trap to fall into as you progress in your career.

Outcome: This particular piece of advice has saved many a senior leader from the quick trip to irrelevance. In my own career, I've used this advice to stay grounded throughout role progression. When I find myself delving too deeply into the minutiae of a company's political environment, I pull back, take a break from the office politicking, and create some provocative content. Works like a charm to help stay grounded and serves as an inspiration to your team.

Brett Ludwig
Vice President,
Communications,
AmerisourceBergen

DON'T BURY THE LEAD.

Most email recipients report email as spam, based solely on the subject line. Don't forget to highlight the important headlines first and call out any specific actions needed.

DO ✓ TAKE THE SUBJECT LINE SERIOUSLY.

With so many emails flying into the average employee's inbox on a given day, a clear, succinct subject line is critical.

TIPS FOR EFFECTIVE USE OF
SUBJECT LINES:

Use a clear subject line that ties to the purpose and call to action of your email. Avoid having your emails ignored. Unclear subject lines create confusion and misunderstanding, and blank subject lines make it difficult for your recipients to navigate their inbox. If your entire message can be captured in a direct subject line, be sure to include EOM (end of message) so recipients know there is no additional content in the body of the note.

Change the subject line on an email thread if it will add clarity. When the topic of a long email thread changes, change the subject line to reflect it, or start a new email if the past history is no longer relevant.

Clearly identify urgent emails. Let your recipient know when an item needs immediate attention by calling it out in the subject line (e.g. URGENT). In the message, be sure to state the rationale for the urgency.

Include a call to action in the subject line, as necessary. If your message requires action on the part of the recipient, note it clearly in the subject line (e.g. ACTION NEEDED).

Inform the recipient when an email is for informational purposes only. (e.g. FYI).

You can also follow the 1-2-3 prioritization rule when sending internal emails to your team. Include the number that corresponds with the level of importance and urgency:

1. Signifies extremely urgent and needs immediate attention

2. Important and requires attention

3. Read and respond at your convenience

Frequently used subject lines

- **URGENT:** Action needed by (date)

- **For Approval:** (Project name)

- **FYI Only/No Action Needed:** (Project Name)

- **Preview or Heads Up:** Advance Copy

- **FYR (For Your Review):** (Project Name)

- (Project Name) **Meeting Prep Materials** (Meeting Date)

- (Project Name) **Report: Updated** (Date)

Due to the nature of our on-the-go society and many remote employees,

68%

of middle managers access work-related email on a smartphone[20]. Consider that mobile devices automatically truncate long subject lines *(> 60 characters)*, so you need to keep it concise to get the recipient's attention.

DON'T GO ON RECIPIENT FISHING TRIPS.

You shouldn't rely on old or expanded distribution lists. Clearly, you don't need to include hundreds of people on an email ultimately intended for only a handful.

DO TARGET THE RIGHT PEOPLE.

To avoid sending the email to people who don't need it, you may need to do a little digging first to find out the right person to contact.

Use group lists only if information is meaningful for the entire group. Ask recipients to please not hit "reply-all" if a response is required and instead respond directly to the sender. Copy supervisors or managers on emails sent to their employee reports so they can be ready to answer questions as needed.

Message   Options

Send   Attach

Tips for Structuring Your Emails

Structure your emails for maximum impact and clarity

Once you've determined that your email is necessary, make it succinct and practical. From the very beginning, write the email as if you were the recipient. Ask:

- Who needs to know?
- What do they need to know?
- Why do they need to know it?

- What's the action I need them to take as a result of the email, and when does it need to be done?

Choose your audience

Using the "To" field

- Use the "To" field to indicate your primary audience. Including someone in the "To" field tells them they are responsible for any follow up, deliverable or next step. Be sensitive to including multiple recipients and the dynamics between individuals. Too many recipients will only result in inaction and more emails requesting clarity on who is doing what.

- Double check that you're sending the message to the correct recipients to avoid any unnecessary embarrassments.

Using the "Cc" field

- Use the "Cc" field as a For Your Information (FYI). The Cc field says "This is an FYI, and you are not expected to take action." Cc your manager when you want him or her to know you've taken an action and use the Cc field sparingly.

Using the "Bcc" field

- Use Bcc for large groups of recipients. Bcc is appropriate when your intent is to Inform and others don't need to know who else is on the list.

- Be judicious in using Bcc on email threads. The feature can keep your supervisor in the loop on projects; but remember, associates who are Bcc'd can respond to the entire chain.

-DON'T-
FAIL TO MONITOR EMAIL VOLUME AND STRESS.

As a leader, you need to know how much email volume is impacting your employees and their stress levels. Ignoring signs of frustration among employees can only lead to burnout and disengagement.

DO ✓

REGULARLY SURVEY EMPLOYEES FOR THEIR VIEWS ON EMAIL VOLUME.

You need to hear from employees to understand what's going on with their email use, and how much stress they may feel. You can either add questions to an existing communication survey or create a separate quick survey on email.

Progressive employers try monitoring the number of hours employees spend on email during their work days as well as on their time off or during vacations. Once levels get too high, it's a clear red flag that something needs to be done to bring things under control.

TAKE THE EMAIL-FREE
VACATION PLEDGE.

To help get you started on the new email you, The Grossman Group created a pledge that will help you unplug and recharge on your next vacation.

1. **I will recognize that it's important for everyone to take time off.** It's how we recharge, reconnect, and get re-energized to be at our best.

2. **I will adjust my mindset and focus on my intention to disconnect.** Going into my vacation, I will plan to not have access to email, and not engage with work. I commit to having a vacation; not a "workcation."

3. **I will set an example.** I will lead by example and model the importance of taking a true vacation for my staff.

4. **I will prepare those with whom I interact regularly.** I will talk with people about how work will be managed in my absence, and that I am looking forward to a much-needed vacation. I will leave detailed status reports with my manager and will set up an out-of-office message with direction on who to contact.

5. **I will be "present" for the right people.** Being present in person and through technology is important for our colleagues when we're at work. It's just as important to be present when we're on vacation. Work can wait a week.

6. **I will share this pledge with my family and those with whom I am vacationing.** I will let them know my plans to disconnect and ask for their support.

7. **I will remind myself that most problems work themselves out.** I will think about those times when I'm not available during working hours. Most often, work problems get figured out without my intervention.

8. **I will resist the urge to re-connect on vacation.** If I'm feeling the need to check email, I will re-read steps 1-5 and re-commit, knowing a change like this is tough, yet takes courage and reaps benefits.

SIGNED _____

DATE _____

DON'T HIT SEND IMMEDIATELY.

First email responses are great as long as they're accurate. Resist the temptation to respond too quickly as you're much more likely to make an embarrassing mistake.

If it's a sensitive note, be especially cautious in your response. Who hasn't received a "nastygram" that really should have been a phone call or discussion in a face-to-face meeting?

DO ✓ CHECK IT TWICE.

Prevent most-embarrassing moments by proofreading everything in an email. This includes the recipient email addresses, message content and any attachments, before you push "send."

If the email relates to a delicate or sensitive issue, consider walking away and revisiting the contents with a fresh perspective before it goes out into the ethers.

EFFECTIVELY USE
ATTACHMENTS:

When possible, include links to files rather than the attachment itself. This saves space in inboxes and the overall system. It also can be helpful if the document may change so readers can access the latest version. Documents can be posted on a SharePoint site or a WorkNet site and linked to in your email.

If you're attaching files, reference them in your message. Don't leave them guessing; let your recipient know if you're sending them files and why.

Consider putting files in formats that typically are smaller in size. For example, PowerPoint can be converted to a PDF file to reduce the size.

Double check that you've included the attachment and that it's the right document. Avoid being embarrassed, or worse, accidentally distributing proprietary information. Are there several versions of the document you're sending in existence? Open it up and make sure you're emailing the most up-to-date version.

Use a recognizable file name for attachments. Choose file names that illustrate the document or content.

Be mindful of version control. If there are several draft versions of a file, add dates to the file name to ensure everyone is working off the same one.

DON'T ⊘ WAIT TO RESPOND.

Too many of us leave senders in the dark, only to have them wondering if the email was even received. Often this happens when the recipient doesn't have an immediate answer. A simple note back telling the recipient you're working on a response goes a long way toward keeping everyone informed and engaged.

DO ✓ CONSIDER THE TIMING.

Email is not an appropriate vehicle for something requiring an urgent response. Keep in mind the audience and the fact that some may not check or respond to email immediately.

EMAIL AND REMOTE WORKERS
DON'T ALWAYS MIX.

Many workers don't have access to email. If they work in a retail or manufacturing environment, chances are only a few employees have regular access to email. In other environments, such as customer service call centors, employees might have easy access to email, but they're not given the time to check it. Keep this in mind as you're trying to reach employees quickly. In some cases, phone calls and meetings are simply the best way to reach an employee.

DON'T 🚫 USE SARCASM, NEGATIVE COMMENTS OR ALL CAPS.

Remember that email messages lack the nuances of voice inflection or facial expressions that are part of personal conversations.

DO ✓ WEIGH POTENTIAL INTERPRETATIONS.

Emails live on forever and can be forwarded, shared, copied and subpoenaed.

Emails can also be misunderstood easily, especially when you commit two of the most frustrating email habits:

- **"SHOUTING" at your colleagues.** Using all capital letters— either for a part of a message or an entire message— distracts from the important nature of your communication.

- **Using emoticons.** They're not professional and they can also lead to confusion—does the smiley face mean you like the idea, or that you're acting on it? Use words and be clear.

DON'T ⊘ LET BAD EMAIL HABITS CONTINUE.

It's clear that email volume can drive down employee morale and productivity. Don't dismiss the important steps you can take to make email work better for you personally and for the people you communicate with.

DO ✓ WORK ON BEING A BETTER EMAIL COMMUNICATOR.

You can start to change your email habits simply by pledging to be better. The result should produce lower overall volume and much clearer communications going forward.

CLOSING

THOUGHT

DON'T

JUST PUT THIS
BOOK
ON
THE
SHELF.

by **DAVID GROSSMAN**
ABC, APR, Fellow PRSA

NO CAPE NEEDED

THE SIMPLEST, SMARTEST, FASTEST STEPS TO IMPROVE
HOW YOU COMMUNICATE BY LEAPS AND BOUNDS

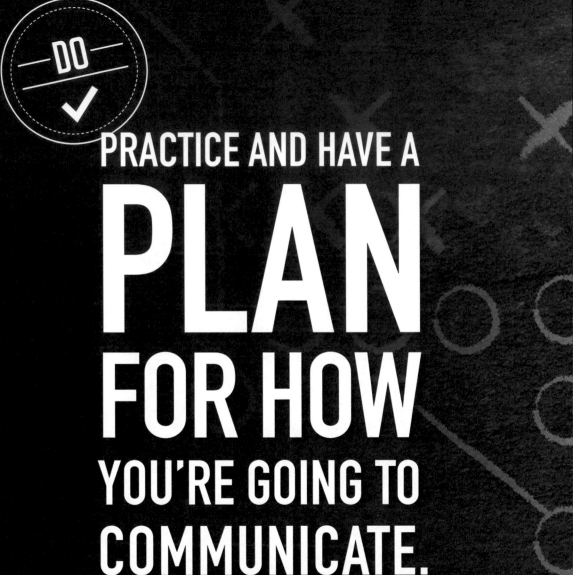

DO ✓

PRACTICE AND HAVE A
PLAN
FOR HOW
YOU'RE GOING TO
COMMUNICATE.

Communication—***done well***—can be tough. But how can you increase the chances that you'll be effective and get what you want? To get good at anything—whether in sports, business, or my latest focus, parenting, you need to work at it.

Experts in anything practice. There's a consistent pattern of effort that successful people apply to the areas in their lives where they want to increase their expertise (and reduce their stress). Even the most successful natural talents, such as Michael Jordan and Bill Gates, became successful because they worked at it. Regularly.

Of course, there's another important ingredient: creating a habit out of communicating in new and more effective ways. And the good news is that experts in psychology tell us that there are proven strategies for making a behavior stick. In other words, it can be done!

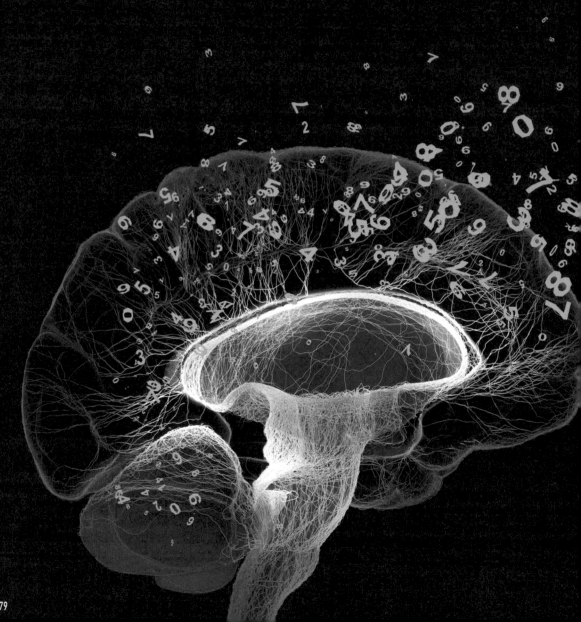

Let's start by debunking a long-held myth. Have you heard that it takes 21 days to form a habit?

That idea came from the research of Maxwell Maltz[21], a cosmetic surgeon who reported in 1960 that it took amputees at least 21 days to stop feeling phantom limb pain, and then speculated that a similar time frame applied to establishing any other type of habit.

In fact, Maltz emphasized that it would take at least 21 days, but researchers in recent years have debunked the idea that 21 days is any magic number. Philippa Lally[22], a health psychology professor at the University College London, said it can take anywhere from:

 18 to 254

days to form a habit, depending on the person and the degree of change that person is seeking.

Lally also pointed out that you shouldn't worry if you fail for a day or two. Instead, she reports that it's more important to embrace the process and commit to a system in which you're continually working to embed the new behavior into your daily life. (In other words, missing one day at the gym doesn't mean you can't be a committed, successful athlete.)

Christine Whelan[23], a public sociologist at the University of Wisconsin-Madison, shared other advice that I found quite helpful in a recent interview with the *Washington Post*, entitled "How to build good habits and actually make them stick."

Here are some highlights from Whelan:

 Once you decide you want to add a behavior, determine which behavior you'll stop to make room for the new action. In other words, what will you stop doing in order to make time for communicating better with your teams?

Change one thing at a time. Don't create a laundry list of things you want to change— it's too overwhelming.

 Go public with your commitment and join a community for support. At minimum, tell someone else what you're working on so they can cheer you on or give you feedback.

Other experts say it's especially important to have a specific action plan. List the goal and pinpoint exactly what you'll do each day or each week to accomplish it. Make sure you then schedule those behaviors in your calendar to ensure that you follow through.

As you can see, just
wanting to change the
way you communicate
won't get the job done.
It's about committing
to it and embracing
the process.

Change may not come in 21 days. Still, as long as you keep working at it, you can transform the way you communicate— and you'll be a stronger, more respected leader because of it.

You might even say you've discovered your own superpower, and there's **NO CAPE NEEDED!**

WOULD YOU LIKE DAVID TO PRESENT A
POWERFUL
PROGRAM
TO YOUR ORGANIZATION?

David Grossman is a sought-after speaker, consultant and executive coach, acclaimed for his highly engaging, interactive, and effective programs. He's known for a thoughtful, personal, and pragmatic approach that leverages communication as one of the ultimate business tools.

From Fortune 500 companies to professional associations and universities, David's proven leadership communication programs benefit leaders at all levels and help them connect the dots between communication and business results.

To invite David to speak to your organization
or team, or for more information, please visit:
www.yourthoughtpartner.com/speaking-and-events

Or contact us directly at **312.829.3252** or
results@yourthoughtpartner.com

DAVID GROSSMAN
ABC, APR, Fellow PRSA

"David helps leaders drive productivity and get the results they want through authentic and courageous leadership and communication."

David is both a teacher and student of effective leadership and communication. He is one of America's foremost authorities on communication and leadership inside organizations, and a sought-after advisor to Fortune 500 leaders.

By acting as an advocate for employees and as a **thought**partner™ to senior management, David helps organizations unleash the power of communication to engage employees and drive performance.

David is Founder and CEO of The Grossman Group, an award-winning Chicago-based communications consultancy focused on organizational consulting, strategic leadership development and internal communications. Clients include Abbott, Baxter, ConAgra Foods, CVS Health, Eastman Chemical, Heinz, Hill-Rom, Johnson & Johnson, Land O'Lakes, Inc., Lockheed Martin, McDonald's, MedStar Health, Microsoft, Motel 6, Nationwide, Rockwell Automation and Tyco, among others.

David is often quoted in media, providing expert commentary and analysis on email in the workplace and employee and leadership issues. He's been featured on "NBC Nightly News," *CBS MoneyWatch*, in the *Chicago Tribune* and the *LA Times*.

Leaders, communication professionals, and educators applaud David's first two books—"You Can't **NOT** Communicate: Proven Communication Solutions That Power the Fortune 100," and its follow up, "You Can't **NOT** Communicate 2"— which continue to receive accolades and praise for reminding leaders—everywhere and at all levels—on the value of getting leadership and communication right.

Twice named *PR Week's* "Boutique Agency of the Year" and *The Holmes Report's* "Employee Communication Agency of the Year," The Grossman Group's work has won all the "Oscars" of communication. The Grossman Group is a certified diversity supplier.

Prior to founding The Grossman Group in 2000, David was director of communications for McDonald's. Currently, he teaches the only graduate-level course on internal communications in the U.S. at Columbia University.

This must-read book highlights the importance of communication in bridging the organization's strategies and goals with an individual's performance. This is the key to making things happen and getting results.

— Norm Wesley, Former Chairman and CEO, Fortune Brands

GET DAVID'S OTHER BOOKS

> Practical, wise, smartly
> designed—an example of what
> it recommends to its readers.

— Jon Iwata, Senior Vice President,
  Marketing and Communications, IBM Corporation

GET CONNECTED

Visit Our Website

Go to **www.yourthoughtpartner.com** to learn more about The Grossman Group and its proven approach to strategic leadership and internal communication. Also download free eBooks such as "Cutting to Win: 6 Steps for Getting Employees on Your Side During Cost Cuts," "How to Think Like a CEO," and "Top 10 Barriers Communicators Face: How to Get Your Leader On Board with Internal Communication."

Contact Us

Are you looking to elevate your team or organization's performance? Call or email us today and we'd be happy to talk about how we can leverage our experience on your behalf. Call **312.829.3252** or email: **Results@yourthoughtpartner.com**

Subscribe to eThoughtStarters

For quick, simple tips to help build better leader**communicators**, subscribe to our **eThoughtStarters** newsletter by visiting **www.yourthoughtpartner.com/ethought-starters.**

Get Quantity Discounts

Books are available at quantity discounts on orders
of 50 copies or more. Please call us at **312.829.3252**,
visit us online at **www.yourthoughtpartner.com/book**
or email us at **office@yourthoughtpartner.com.**

Book David to Speak at Your Event

To help your leaders be better communicators, invite
David to speak to groups large and small by going to
www.yourthoughtpartner.com/speaking-and-events.

Stay Connected

Thousands of readers continue to receive communication
tools and best practices from David. You can do so
too, by subscribing to the leader**communicator blog**
(www.yourthoughtpartner.com/blog) or by following David:

@ThoughtPartner   **http://on.fb.me/1b6ZZEz**   **http://linkd.in/1L3iw43**

{ REFERENCES

1. Ketchum, "Leadership Communication Monitor Study" (2013)

2. Towers Watson, "Engagement at Risk: Driving Strong Performance in a Volatile Global Environment," Global Workforce Study (2012)

3. Towers Watson, "Global Workforce Study" (2014)

4. Towers Watson, "Change and Communication ROI Study" (2013-2014)

5. Towers Watson, "Communication ROI Study" (2009-2010)

6. Towers Watson, "WorkUSA Survey" (2008/2009)

7. Psychologically Healthy Workplace Program, "American Psychology Association Harrison Interactive" Workplace Survey (2012)

8. Towers Watson, "WorkUSA Survey" (2008/2009)

9. Harvard Business Review, "Collective Genius" (2014)

10. Wall Street Journal, "What Do Workers Want From the Boss?" (2015)

11. Psychology Today, "Is Nonverbal Communication a Numbers Game?" (2011)

12. Harvard Business Review, "How to Give a Killer Presentation" (2013)

13. Forbes, "Cisco's Obsession With Presentation Skills Makes Managers Better Leaders" (2014)

14. Forbes, "The CEO as Storyteller in Chief" (2009)

15. Forbes, "How to Use Storytelling as a Leadership Tool" (2012)

16. Harvard Business Review, "Storytelling That Moves People" (2003)

17. The Conference Board, "Job Satisfaction: 2014 Edition" (2014)

18. Research conducted for a client by The Grossman Group (2014)

19. Fortune, "Stop Checking Email Now" (2012)

20. The Grossman Group, "Work-Related Email Perception Study" (2012)

21. Forbes, "Habit Formation: The 21 Day Myth" (2013)

22. Wiley Online Library, European Journal of Social Psychology Abstract (2009)

23. Washington Post, "How to Build Good Habits—and Actually Make Them Stick" (2015)

NO CAPE NEEDED

THE SIMPLEST, SMARTEST, FASTEST STEPS TO IMPROVE
HOW YOU COMMUNICATE BY LEAPS AND BOUNDS

by **DAVID GROSSMAN** ABC, APR, Fellow PRSA